CHOOSING SIDES

(Grades 6-8)

By Lotunja A. Wright

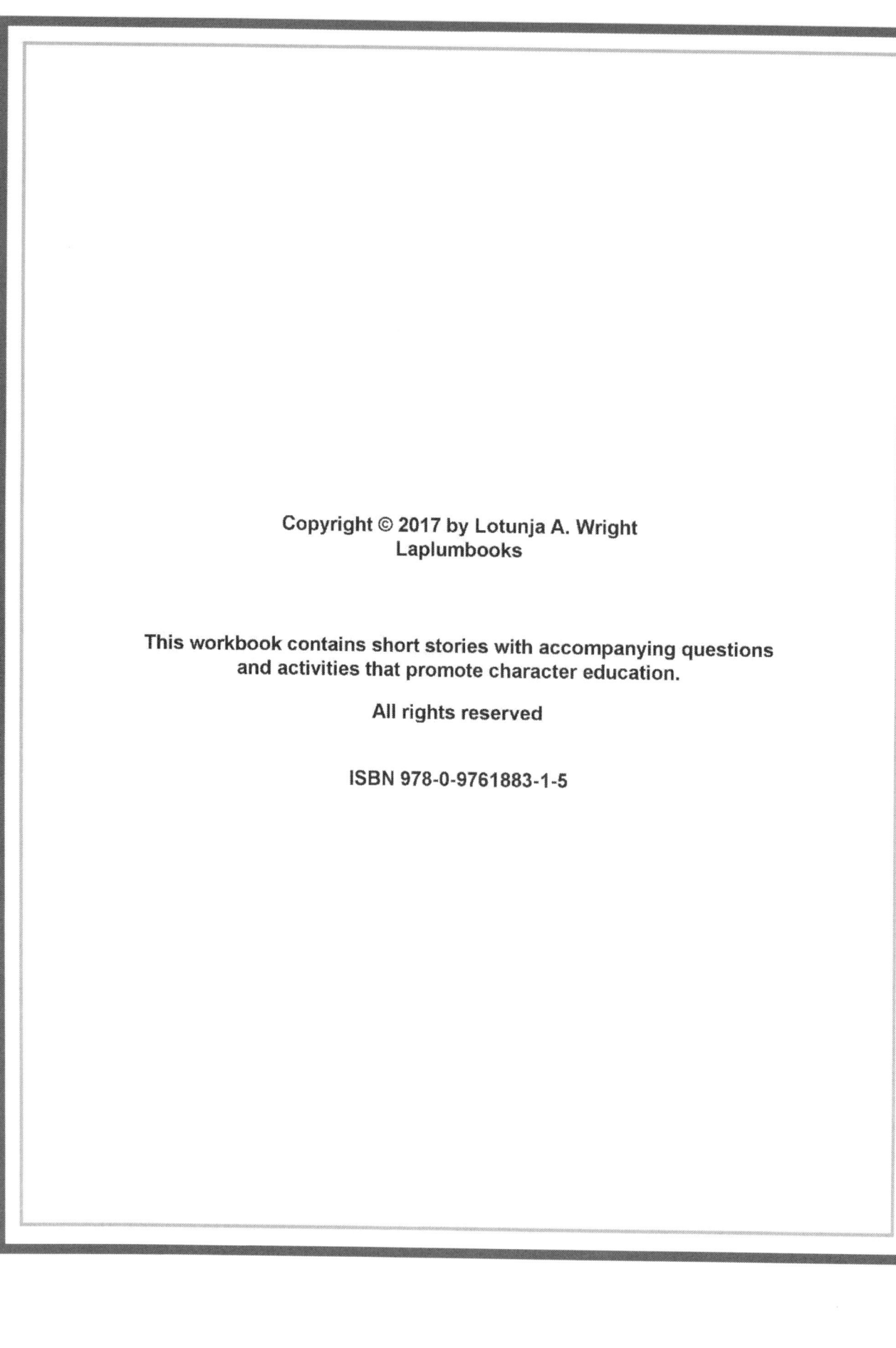

This workbook contains short stories with accompanying questions
and activities that promote character education.

ISBN 978-0-9761883-1-5

TABLE OF CONTENTS

Introduction

Life is all about making choices. In middle school, you may be faced with making some difficult and possibly grown-up choices. Within the pages of this workbook, you will be able to gain insight into both the benefits of making good choices and the adversity that follows when willfully making bad choic es. At some point, we all must choose a side. Good or bad.

Girls, please turn to page two.

Guys, please turn to page seven.

Just Us Girls

Which statement do you identify with the most? Be honest and circle the statement that best represents you.

1.

"She started it, but I'm going to finish it! People just get on my nerves!"

2.

"She's so cool. She's always studying. She's funny, teachers love her, and she's pretty!"

If you identified with statement number one, what do you think about girls who fight and argue?

_____

_____

_____

_____

If you fight or argue a lot or know someone who does, does fighting and arguing really solve problems or lead to bigger problems?

_____

_____

_____

_____

If you identify with statement number two, what have you done to to be considered that way? Explain.

_____
_____
_____
_____
_____

There was once a popular song where the singer stated that he started from the bottom, but he made it to the top. Moving from the bottom can mean many different things to many different people, and within various communities the meaning and values that define both bottom and top can also be different.

Successful girls and women work hard, study hard, focus on the positive aspects of life, and help others. But yet, some girls feel like being positive will not gain them any popularity. Besides, many of the reality stars of today are very negative, but they get great ratings. How can that be explained? Well, many people are attracted to drama, but just because that may be the case, drama seeking isn't usually a great path to follow when striving for a truly successful life.

Research opportunity:

Go online, search, and read about six successful women in business, technology, government, finance, film, and media. (One person from each category.) List their information below.

Name_____

Profession_____

Interesting Fact _____

Name_____

Profession_____

Interesting Fact _____

Name_____

Profession_____

Interesting Fact _____

Name_____

Profession_____

Interesting Fact _____

Name_____

Profession_____

Interesting Fact _____

Name_____

Profession_____

Interesting Fact _____

Why would it be important to know about women who are successful in various careers?

_____
_____
_____
_____
_____

What words come to mind when you think about the women you have researched?

_____
_____
_____
_____
_____

Do you think they could have accomplished their dreams if they always behave negatively?

Yes or No (Circle One)

Do you think these women are good role models? Why or why not?

_____
_____
_____
_____
_____

Do you see anything in your personality and/or behavior that may be similar to the women you researched or what positive personality traits do you have?

_____
_____
_____
_____
_____
_____

If you see any things in your personality and/or behavior that are not positive, what are they and how can you change those things?

_____
_____
_____
_____
_____

What can your teachers, parents, counselors, and other adults in your life do to help you with that change?

_____
_____
_____
_____
_____

How do you think your parents, and other people who love you, feel when you behave in an inappropriate manner? How do your loved ones feel when you do good things?

_____

_____

_____

_____

_____

What are examples of positive traits and behaviors? List three positive traits or behaviors you have seen in other people.

_____

_____

_____

_____

Draw an image of how you see your life in ten years.

What will it take to create the life you see for yourself?

GIRLS, PLEASE PROCEED TO PAGE FOURTEEN

Just Us Boys

Which statement do you identify with the most? Be honest and circle the statement that best represents you.

1. "That dude is a punk! Look at him studying. He's just a book bag-wearing punk!"

2. "I'm the dude who studies, and gets good grades. I'm respectful and I'm cool. One day, I'm going to change lives, and earn way more money than those thugs can ever get their hands on."

If you identified with statement number one, do you think it's cool to devalue education? Why or why not?

_____

_____

_____

_____

_____

If you identify with statement number two, what have you done to consider yourself that way?

_____

_____

_____

_____

_____

There was once a popular song where the singer stated that he started from the bottom, but he made it to the top. Moving from the bottom can mean many different things to many different people, and within various communities the meaning and values that define both bottom and top can also be different.

Successful boys and men work hard, study hard, focus on the positvie aspects in life, and help others. Some guys avoid being positive because they may not think it's cool to be a positive person. If you look at any truly successful person, the formula for their success is usually the same. They add confidence, a positive attitude, and a great work ethic to to equal goal achievement and success.

Research opportunity:

Go online, search, and read about six successful men in business, technology, government, finance, film, and media. (One person from each category.) List their information below.

Name_____

Profession_____

Interesting Fact _____

Name_____

Profession_____

Interesting Fact _____

Name_____

Profession_____

Interesting Fact _____

Name_____

Profession_____

Interesting Fact_____

Name_____

Profession_____

Interesting Fact _____

Name_____

Profession_____

Interesting Fact_____

Why would it be important to know about men who are successful in various careers?

_____

_____

_____

_____

_____

What words come to mind when you read about these men?

_____
_____
_____
_____

Do you think those men became as successful as they are by continuously walking down destructive paths such as being dishonest, selling drugs or other prohibited items, fighting, and stealing? **Yes or No (Circle One)**

Do you think these guys are good role models? **Yes or No**

Why or Why not?

_____
_____
_____
_____
_____

Do you think boys who devalue education and are disrespectful to others are good role models for you? Why or why not?

_____
_____
_____
_____
_____

Many people claim that clothing affects behavior. Do you agree or disagree with this idea? Please explain.

_____

_____

_____

_____

What kind of jobs or careers do you think boys and men who sag their pants and dress sloppily will be able to obtain? Explain.

_____

_____

_____

_____

_____

_____

Do you believe drug dealers, con men, and thieves, live long, prosperous lives? Why or why not?

_____

_____

_____

_____

_____

Do you think it's better to live a destructive and short life, but make a lot of money, or to live a long life with integrity filled with family, friends, and fun? Please explain.

Side note: *Most people who obtain their money in dishonest ways, either don't make a lot of money or will not be able to keep their money, compared to people who have honest careers and jobs.*

_____

_____

_____

_____

If you see any things in your personality and/or behavior that are not positive, what are they? Please be honest.

_____

_____

_____

_____

_____

How can you change those things?

_____

_____

_____

_____

What can your teachers, parents, counselors, and other adults in your life do to help you with that change?

_____

_____

_____

_____

How do you think your parents and other people who love you feel when you behave in an inappropriate manner? How do your loved ones feel when you do good things?

_____

_____

_____

_____

_____

What are examples of positive traits and behaviors? List three positive traits or behaviors you have seen in other people.

_____

_____

_____

_____

_____

Draw an image of how you see your life in ten years.
What will it take to create the life you see for yourself?

Chapter Two

Temperature's Rising

"Shena, close the door behind you please," Mrs. Wilson asked a tardy Shena Crawford. This was only Shena's fifth day at her new school, Hamilton High, and she had already been tardy twelve times just that week.

"Close it yourself," Shena snapped.

"Sweetheart, there is no need to be rude." Mrs. Wilson spoke softly, attempting to calm the situation.

"Whatever," Shena responded and brushed past the flabbergasted teacher to a seat on the opposite side of the room from her assigned seat.

"Young lady, I will not have you talking to me like that. Go to the office now!" Mrs. Wilson rushed to the door and flung it open, hoping that this gesture would show Shena that she meant business. Turning away from the teacher, Shena started talking to the girl sitting next to her, totally ignoring Mrs. Wilson. Shena had been rude and disrespectful all week, and the teacher had let it slide, but today was Friday, and Mrs. Wilson had had enough.

"Get out, NOW!" Mrs. Wilson yelled. She left the door and rushed over to where Shena confidently sat. Looking up at a snarling Mrs. Wilson standing over her, a smug Shena took her time rising from her seat and moved slowly towards the door. "This classroom smells funny anyway. I can't wait to get outta here," a defiant Shena retorted, determined to have the last word.

Mrs. Wilson stood quietly, waiting for Shena to exit the room. When Shena got to the threshold of the door, she turned around and flipped her middle finger up at Mrs. Wilson who had already turned to face the class. The gesture made the class erupt with laughter. After Shena finally left, it took Mrs. Wilson ten minutes to get the class calm enough to begin their lesson. The teacher just shook her head in frustration. They had lost fifteen minutes of instructional time, just dealing with Shena's attitude.

Not caring what the teacher or anyone else thought, Shena walked down the hall in her stylish, bedazzled A-line t-shirt and short jean skirt. Short skirts were prohibited at school, but Shena couldn't have cared less. No one was going to challenge her. All the teachers had heard about her short fuse, and because it was the end of the year, they chose to look the other way and ignore the dress code violation. They had bigger school violations to worry about.

Instead of going to the principal's office as Mrs. Wilson had instructed, Shena made a detour to the girls' bathroom. She hadn't had a smoke since walking to school that morning, and her internal smoke alarm told her that it was time for another one.

In the bathroom, the dingy grey walls were covered with so much writing that the true color was barely visible, and chewing gum had been used to dot an occasional 'i' or 'j' in someone's name. The wall was ugly, but unimportant, so Shena leaned against it, and rummaged through her purse to find a cigarette. She didn't care about the yucky wall as long as she could hurry up and take a puff of cigarette smoke into her lungs.

At thirteen, she was already addicted to cigarettes, and the one she held between her lips filled her with pleasure as she touched the lighter to its tip. As she began to breathe the vile cigarette smoke in and out, she flinched when she heard a toilet flush. She had thought she was alone. The sound of the toilet flushing put her on high alert and she slipped her hand behind her back. Only a few girls at the school could be trusted not to tell the principal on her. If it wasn't one of them, it was better to hide the evidence of her "crime." Shena knew that if she got kicked out of school again, because she was already on parole, she'd face some pretty tough consequences.

Coming out of the stall in full uniform, even though the school had done away with uniforms the previous year, was one of the worst do-gooders in the school, Melissa Grant. Even though getting a pass to the restroom during class time was almost impossible for any other student, Melissa always seemed to be able to snag a pass. Melissa was on the hall monitor team for their grade level. She was always running errands for teachers and helping out in the library or front office, and worst of all, she was always in other students' business.

As Melissa thoroughly washed her hands, she looked in Shena's direction. "Do I smell smoke?"

Shena pressed her lips together to hide the smile. Did this goody-goody think she was going to get an answer? Really?

Melissa squinted her eyes and wrinkled her nose as she quickly turned off the water while examining Shena for the source of the smoke.

Shena still held the cigarette behind her back. Not because she feared Melissa, but so that she could enjoy the rest of her smoke break. "Little girl, keep moving. It's all good in here," was Shena's nonchalant response.

"I know I smell smoke, and I know you have a cigarette. Let me see it," Melissa demanded as she took a pen and a small pad out of her hall monitor's smock. All of the hall monitors were trained to document any offense with the date, time, and location, but most importantly, they had to actually see the incident. If Shena didn't produce the cigarette, Melissa couldn't prove the incident. Determined, she tried to look behind Shena's back because it was apparent that that was where the cigarette was hidden. When Melissa moved, Shena turned her body so that Melissa couldn't see. After several attempts, it was clear Shena was making a game of blocking Melissa's view.

Frustrated, Melissa finally grabbed Shena's cigarette-holding arm. Although there were numerous rumors about Shena's temper during her first week of school, they didn't scare Melissa. She took her oath to serve the school very seriously. She was determined to see the cigarette and to report it to the administrators.

Shena had humored Melissa's tactics to see the cigarette, but Melissa's grabbing her arm took things to a totally different level. Reacting, Shena slapped Melissa's face so hard that a hair-raising echo could be heard throughout the large restroom, and beyond. Melissa's face immediately turned red and stung with pain. Surprised, she pressed her hand against her cheek in an attempt to subdue the pain.

Shocked, Melissa backed away from Shena, fearing what might come next, but it was already too late. Shena had red in her eyes as she descended on Melissa like a rabid dog, spitting fury, punching and kicking, as Melissa begged her to stop. Falling over her own feet, Melissa fell to the hard tile floor, still trying to fight back. Shena was too quick for her and always managed to block Melissa's hands before they reached her body. Grabbing hard, locking her fingers in the other girl's hair, Shena bashed Melissa's head on the floor, and blood splattered both girls' clothes.

Melissa screamed out in pain a few times until she quickly learned that yelling only provoked harder hits. When hitting Melissa seemed to bore her, Shena began stabbing Melissa with the pen she'd carried earlier; the pen she would have used to document the incident. Curling her battered body into a ball, suffering from the shock of the stabbing, Melissa could no longer make a sound. She just lay there, taking the abuse as if she were frozen.

Finally satisfied, Shena dropped the bloody pen and got to her feet. Backing away from Melissa, she yelled, "You don't ever touch me!"

Melissa just moaned.

Mrs. Randall, a teacher whose classroom was next door to the girls' restroom, heard the shouting and went towards the restroom to see what all the commotion was about. Entering, she collided with Shena, who was running away from the scene of her crime. Before seeing Melissa, Mrs. Randall said to Shena, "An excuse me would be nice." Shena looked into Mrs. Randall's face, but ran full force through the doors without saying a word.

Wondering about Shena's bloody shirt, the teacher stepped through the doors. Upon rounding the corner of the restroom, Mrs. Randall could clearly see what Shena was running from. She saw a bleeding Melissa sprawled out in the middle of the dirty restroom floor, sound finally coming from her, as though Shena's flight had released the mute button holding Melissa's vocal cords. Melissa wailed pitifully when she saw Mrs. Randall.

"Melissa, did Shena do this to you?" Mrs. Randall asked, as if there were any other possibility.

"Yes," Melissa managed between snotty sobs.

"Where are you hurt?" Mrs. Randall continued, trying to inspect Melissa's head wounds.

"Head, fa..face, arms, sto...stomach," was Melissa's labored response.

"Don't move?" Mrs. Randall demanded. "Sit still," Mrs. Randell softened her tone to almost a whisper as if the softness of her voice could somehow counteract the pain Melissa felt.

Mrs. Randall tried to comfort Melissa as she knelt down to the dirty floor and stroked her hair in an effort to soothe her. Trying to keep the girl from losing con- sciousness was hard, because it seemed like Melissa desperately wanted to slip away from her terror and pain.

"Look!" Six talkative girls, having their restroom break, crowded into the room at the same time. Wide-eyed and instantly curious, they stared and held their collective breath.

They were from Mrs. Wilson's class, but before they could ask any questions, Mrs. Randall yelled, "Go get help! Run to the front office!"

Four of the girls ran full speed out of the restroom and straight to the front office, while two others went back to class to inform Mrs. Wilson of what happened. Soon after, the principal, both assistant principals, the school resource officer, and a male P.E. coach ran into the girls' bathroom with walkie-talkies. One of the assistant principals was talking in a low tone to someone on the walkie-talkie. It almost seemed like a joke because everyone she could have been talking to was piled into the restroom. All the teachers and administrators focused on getting Melissa to talk so that she wouldn't lose consciousness.

Soon, the Emergency Medical Technicians burst into the bathroom, escorted by Ms. Rockledge, the school secretary. Students from several classes spilled from classroom doors, watching as the EMTs moved the stretcher transporting Melissa down the hallway. Full of speculation about what had happened, noisy students were funneled back into their classrooms at the urging of their teachers, as the doors closed behind the EMTs and Melissa.

Everyone grew silent at the sound of the ambulance siren, and in Mrs. Wilson's classroom, no one said what so many of them were thinking. But, with the name, Shena Crawford, scrawled boldly across his clipboard, the Principal looked determined. Striding away from the main office with the school resource officer, and one of the assistant principals in tow, he left the hallway in search for Shena. Thirty minutes later, they found her hiding under the bleachers in the gym ... still smoking.

Shena went to the police station in handcuffs – without her cigarettes. She was expelled from school, and Melissa's parents pressed charges against her for aggravated assault. Shena would never attend that school or possibly any other regular school again. Stabbing someone is attempted murder, and the severity of her punishment would depend on the judge.

A week later, Melissa still had not come back to school. She had been injured worse than originally thought. Shena had broken Melissa's collar bone, and given her a concussion. The beating had ruptured her pelvis, stabbed her in the head, and nearly severed an artery in her wrist; the bleeding from the artery alone might have killed Melissa.

In the emergency room, the doctors were in disbelief that Melissa's injuries could have been caused by another 13-year old girl in a school fight. Whether the medical team believed it or not, it happened and Melissa suffered tremendously as a result of an out of control bully.

Melissa's friends tried talking to her to cheer her up, but her depression surrounding her injuries was so deep that no one could spend more than a few minutes on the phone with her. Her body was bruised and wounded, but her spirit seemed to be devastated. According to her friends, she would heal physically one day, but the mental anguish would last much longer. All because she just wanted to do the right thing.

Discussion Questions

(Discuss your thoughts with an adult or peer mentor.)

1.   Because Melissa grabbed Shena's arm first, do you think she deserved to be beaten and stabbed? Why or why not?

2.   Do you think that hurting Melissa was worth the consequences that Shena will have to face? Why or why not?

3.   How could Shena have handled this situation differently?

4.   Have you ever hurt someone in a fight? Did fighting that person solve the problem or create more problems for you?

5.   If you answered yes to number 4, what were your consequences for fighting? Do you think the punishment was fair?

6. If Shena had killed Melissa, depending on the law, she might be facing murder charges with adult consequences. Then, two families, Shena's and Melissa's, would be hurting. Is anger ever worth doing something so bad that two families will be destroyed? Why or why not?

7. Because Shena was already on parole, why do you think she choose to get in trouble again?

8. List three positive ways to deal with anger or rage?

Chapter Three

Coded!

Use the characters below to decode the sayings.

A=☺☺ B=≠ C=ℒ D=π E=∍ F=≥ G=± H=£ I=¥ J=ℋ K=◊ L=◠ M=⅄ N=୪
O=□ P=ƨ Q=● R=ⱶ S=○ T=ⱬ U=ⱴ V=∫ W=↓ X=↕ Y=∏ Z=₪

---

1. £□୪∍○ⱬ∏   ≠ⱴ¥◠πο   ℒ£☺☺ⱶ☺☺ℒⱬ∍ⱶ

   _ _ _ _ _ _   _ _ _ _ _   _ _ _ _ _ _ _ _ _

2. ↓□ⱶ◊   ୪□↓, ƨ◠☺☺∏   ◠☺☺ⱬ∍ⱶ

   _ _ _ _   _ _ _'   _ _ _ _   _ _ _ _ _

3. ο◠☺☺ℒⱶο   ୪□↓   ƨ☺☺∏   ◠☺☺ⱬ∍ⱶ

   _ _ _ _ _ _   _ _ _'   _ _ _   _ _ _ _ _

4. ⱬⱶ∍☺☺ⱬ   □ⱬ£∍ⱶο   ☺☺ο   ∏□ⱴ   ↓☺☺୪ⱬ   ⱬ□   ≠∍   ⱬⱶ∍☺☺ⱬ∍π

   _ _ _ _ _   _ _ _ _ _ _ _   _ _ _   _ _ _   _ _ _ _   _ _   _ _   _ _ _ _ _ _ _

5. ℒ£☺☺୪±∍   ⱬ£∍   ↓□ⱶ◠π   ≥□ⱶ   ⱬ£∍   ≠∍ⱬⱬ∍ⱶ

   _ _ _ _ _ _   _ _ _   _ _ _ _ _   _ _ _   _ _ _   _ _ _ _ _ _

Topic: Honesty

Chapter Four

The Shoes

"Terrell, man, you know we're gonna get caught, why do you wanna do this?" Justin Bridges frowned up at his best friend since elementary school.

"I saw Coach Scott put the new basketball shoes in the storage room out back. Man, just be quiet and we can get paid selling these bad boys on the street."

"Dude, how do you know we won't get caught?" Chance asked his friend.

"'Cause, I just know. Coach goes down to the elementary school every day after school to pick up his kids and take them to the babysitter. He won't be back here 'til around 4:45. We got time." Terrell said, confident in himself. His voice was as cool as the cool blue letterman's jacket he wore. He had jacked it from a timid boy in the band. Everyone knew the jacket didn't belong to Terrell, but no one said anything.

"It's not just about Coach Scott. What if another teacher catches us? We could go to jail." Chance was really worried. He'd never stolen anything in his life. His mom made sure of that. She taught him that his great grandfather had been shot and killed because he stole another man's horse. She taught him this lesson every chance she had after she'd caught Chance trying to take cash out of the church collection plate when he was nine.

"Look, if it makes you feel any better, punk, wait out here," Terrell sneered. Without any more argument, Chance reluctantly waited at the storage room door.

Terrell had been in the storage room for five minutes, when Amber Moore, cheerleading captain, came bouncing by the back gate of the school. At first, she didn't see Chance, but on second glance, she saw him and decided to go check him out.

"Whatcha doing back here Chance, being weird?" She laughed.

"I'm just waiting on somebody."

"All the way back here?"

Chance looked away. He was a really bad liar, and knew that if he looked into Amber's deep brown eyes, he'd tell her everything. He'd had a crush on Amber since the 6th grade, but now that they were 9th graders, he had moved on.

"Yeah, well, I thought I saw some loose change on the ground, so I came back here to see." Chance pretended to search the ground for non-existent change, then shrugged. "Guess I was wrong; nothing here. See you later Amber," Chance said, as he ran off, hoping she'd leave so that she wouldn't see Terrell coming out the back.

"But…" Amber started, but Chance had run out of earshot.

Chance stopped at the front steps of the school and waited until he saw Amber bounce off in the opposite direction. When he saw that the coast was clear, he ran back to check on his partner.

When there was still no sign of Terrell, Chance began to panic. It had been fifteen minutes now, and Terrell hadn't come out yet. It started to dawn on Chance that when Terrell did come out, they would need to find a place to store the shoes. Where would they be able to hide all those boxes of shoes? Looking over his shoulder, he saw that there were still some students in the front of the building and Chance knew that those students just made for a bigger problem.

Even though Chance and Terrell were in the back of the building, a fence prevented them from going out that way. They'd have to go back up front to leave the premises and Chance was sure the kids waiting on their rides would see them and report it to a teacher. In the midst of Chance's thoughts of their troubled getaway, Terrell emerged from the storage room with empty hands.

"See, I told you you couldn't get those shoes." An almost relieved Chance immediately went in on Terrell.

"Nope, you're wrong. I've got 'em." Terrell smiled.

"Where?"

"They're at the back door."

"Back door? What back door?" Chance was confused.

"There's a back door in the storage room." Terrell replied.

"Okay, so there's a back door. We can't get to them out without the people around the school seeing us; and plus, where are we going to put them? Just come on. Let's go!" Chance pleaded.

"Nope, you're wrong again man. I cut a hole in the fence behind the storage room, and it's big enough for us to get through. We'll have to crawl, but it's all good. It will be worth it when we get money for the shoes." Terrell's voice was still steady as if he had everything figured out and under control.

Even though it was a cool, fall day, Chance felt hot inside, and he started to sweat. He couldn't leave his boy hanging like that, so he was actually going to have to go through with stealing the shoes.

"Come on man, let's make this fast." Chance gave in. After ten minutes of getting all of the shoes through the little hole Terrell had made for them, the boys stashed many of them in the woods behind the school so they could come back later and get the rest of the shoes.

"I'll get my brother to bring us here later to get the rest," Terrell offered, still cool as a cucumber. "My brother will want a cut of the money, but we'll be alright 'cause we're gonna sell all of these bad boys!" That was the first sign of emotion Chance had heard in Terrell's voice and the first bit of emotion he had seen in his face the entire time. Terrell was grinning mischievously. Chance was suddenly more nervous because his friend was not nervous at all.

The plan was executed exactly as Terrell had planned – without any problems. They went back later that afternoon with Terrell's brother, Chad, a tenth grader. Chad only had a learner's permit and shouldn't have been driving without a licensed driver in the car, but he drove everywhere he needed to go in their mother's car while she slept the day away after pulling a 12-hour night shift at Longview Hospital.

Terrell was smart and even had a storage spot picked out for the shoes. Everything was going according to plan, but that night, Chance couldn't sleep. He tossed and turned thinking about that evening's events. He even woke up and called Terrell.

But, Terrell was sound asleep. When he answered the phone, Chance was sorry he had even called. Terrell was no comfort to him.

Chance kept having dreams of his great grandfather getting shot because of stealing a horse. Although Chance had not been there when it happened, he was there in his dream, and every time he walked over to see his grandfather lying on the ground in his dream, it wasn't his grandfather that he'd see, but himself lying in a pool of blood. Dead on the cold, hard, unforgiving ground. In the dream, he had been shot and according to what the people around him were saying, it was over some sneakers. The sneakers he and Terrell had stolen.

Chance woke up in a cold sweat each time he had that dream, which made it a really rough night for him. It was so hard to sleep that after the fourth time he'd had that dream, he just decided to stay awake for the rest of the night.

The next day, Chance's eyes were bloodshot. It looked like he'd been out partying all night. When he caught up with Terrell in front of the school, Terrell looked happy and well-rested.

"Man, I couldn't sleep last night," Chance confided.

"Don't punk out on me now. We have our ticket to a lot of extra cash in our hands, and you're not gonna throw it away for me." Terrell gave Chance a long cold stare, making his point before he disappeared into the sea of students entering the school.

Chance felt tired. More tired than he already felt after a sleepless night. He thought he might collapse if he didn't yell at his legs to keep standing. Even though he didn't remember walking, he was finally able to find his way into the school. The first person he saw when he got into the school was Amber Moore.

"Did you hear?" Amber dismally asked Chance.

"Hear what?" Chance didn't stop to talk to her. He kept walking as though he was on a mission, but even he didn't know where he was going.

"Everybody's talking about it. Somebody stole all of the basketball team's new shoes!" Amber explained without taking a single breath. "The team refuses to play until the thief returns their shoes, or someone buys them new ones. We were going to be going to the championship this year. Everyone was looking forward to it. Now, we may not even have a team any more. This sucks." Amber said, shaking her head.

Chance brushed past Amber, almost knocking her over.

"Hey!" She called out.

"Sorry Amber. I've got to go." Chance responded.

"Weirdo!" She yelled after him.

Chance rushed past all the kids in the hallway who all seemed to be talking about the theft. He stopped dead in his tracks when he heard an announcement from the principal asking for anyone who had information about the theft to come forward.

After the principal finished his announcement, Chance continued on with his task. With determination on his face and in his eyes, he barged past the loud kids in the hall, including Terrell who was perched on the staircase by the principal's office. Looking at the deceitful smirk on Terrell's face, Chance knew there was only one thing left for him to do.

The two boys exchanged cold stares for what seemed like forever. With his eyes, Terrell seemed to say, "Don't mess this up man." Disregarding his childhood friend's silent warning, Chance quickly rushed into the principal's office unannounced.

Swallowing hard, Chance gathered enough nerve to say the words he'd wanted to say at midnight, when he couldn't sleep because of all the bad dreams. He started, "Mr. Walden, I have something I need to tell you …" With his next breath, his next words, Chance felt the burden of theft, feeling like a ton of bricks, fall away.

Discussion Questions

(Discuss your thoughts with an adult or peer mentor.)

1.   Define HONOR.

2.   Define CONSCIENCE.

3.   Define MORAL(S).

4.   Should Chance tell Principal Walden about Terrell or should he take all the blame? Why or why not?

5.   Why do you think Chance went through with helping Terrell steal the shoes?

6.   Do you think Chance should have done anything differently?

7.   In real life, how does stealing affect those who are stolen from?

8.   What would you do if you were in this situation?

9.   If someone stole from you, and someone else knew about it, would you want them to tell? Or, would you want them to be loyal to the thief for the principle of not "snitching?"

10.   Why would Chance feel relieved to tell the principal about the theft?

11.   Would you tell, if you knew about a theft?

Chapter Five

Kari

"Give me some gum! If my mama smells this alcohol on me, she's going to tear into me like a shark into fresh meat!" Bleary-eyed, Davon Martin pleaded with his friend, Blue. Blue was a Miller Creek High School dropout, and Davon was in grave danger of following the same path, if he didn't get himself together.

Blue took another sip of the beer they had bought at the corner store, and laid back on the gray seats of the Blue Honda Accord. The tinted windows were so dark that it would have been hard to see what they were doing in the car in the daytime, let alone at night. They had drank a 12 pack of beer.

"Man, it's cool. Your mama won't smell a thing," Blue slurred.

Too drunk to care, Davon leaned back and let his eyes close. "My mom is always flipping out. She needs to start treating me like a man."

"I know, man. My mom tried that junk with me a few years ago ... kept it up until I laid down the law and let her know I wasn't having it." After a long pause, he continued, "That's probably what you need to do, man."

"What?" Davon opened his eyes and blinked.

"Lay down the law! Are you on Mars or something? I just gave you the best advice of your life and you ask, 'What'?" Blue looked over at his friend.

Davon turned to look out of the window, and got lost in his cloudy thoughts feeling exactly like he was really on Mars or something.

****

Kari Brooks was packing for her weekend at the University of Georgia. She had worked so hard throughout high school to get good grades. She was the Senior Class President, and active in the drama club, the band, and the Beta Club. She had always been extremely active during her high school years so that she would have her pick of colleges, and, she had succeeded. She had been accepted at Georgia State, the University of Georgia, Spelman College, and Hampton University. She and her friend Vanessa had both been accepted to the University of Georgia, and they were looking forward to spending the weekend on campus with other upcoming freshmen. She had just finished packing her pink bejeweled tank top and blue jean shorts when her mom came into her room.

"Hey, baby. You almost finished packing?"

Ms. Brooks was so proud of her daughter. She had struggled so hard to make sure Kari and her little brother had everything they needed after Mr. Books walked out on them. She was at every PTA meeting and made sure to help Kari and her little brother as much as she could with their homework. Mrs. Brooks was a college graduate herself, and she knew the hard work it would take for her children to become successful. She knew that if she hadn't graduated from college, she and her children wouldn't be as comfortable as they were.

"Yes, Mom. I'm almost finished. Vanessa will be here in about thirty minutes to pick me up."

Mrs. Brooks laughed, "I love you, my child, but you should have been packed yesterday. You are the Princess of Procrastination."

"And, you're the Queen!" Kari joked.

"Watch it!" Her mom leaned against the doorframe and smiled. "Alright sweetheart, I'll be a phone call away if you need me."

"Yes, Mommy, dear." Kari made puppy dog eyes at her mother. They teased each other this way often. They had a mother/daughter relationship that many people envied. Mrs. Brooks didn't act like a "friend" more than a mother, but Kari knew she could talk to her mom about anything, and she could count on her for good advice. Mrs. Brooks was definitely a strong mother, but she made sure to balance her strength with empathy for her children.

"Mom, I'll only be an hour away. You could walk there if you wanted to."

Mrs. Brooks smiled at that and quietly left her daughter to her packing.

****

"Dae!" Blue yelled. Dae was Davon's nickname with his friends.

"What's up, man?"

"We fell asleep. We need to get out of here, before the police decide to drop by and be nosey."

"Go, then. Why'd you wake me up?"

"'Because you're gonna drive."

"No I won't. I can't ... You have to drive!"

"Dae, that's not right." Blue rubbed his eyes. Shaking his head, he turned the key in the ignition and proceeded to crank up the car. With a flutter, the engine turned and Blue steered the blue Honda into a U-turn out of the deserted parking lot where they had been parked for the last two hours.

From the swerving of the car, it was apparent that Blue didn't need to be driving, but Davon was too drunk to realize it. His head was cocked to the side, eyes closed, as he relaxed, enjoying the bliss of his intoxication ... not knowing the danger he was in.

The yellow line couldn't be seen between the two lanes because it was continuously underneath their car. Blue was too inebriated to know or care that he was not on the right side of the road. Blue didn't notice, but the police, who were parked at the top of the hill, definitely noticed. They immediately put on their blue lights.

Those lights were like blue electricity that jolted Blue to the point of almost sobering him. It sobered him enough to make him think that he needed to speed up. He knew with his juvenile arrest record, he couldn't afford to be caught drunk. He knew he would spend a long time in juvenile detention, maybe even be charged as an adult this time. He'd been there before, and he refused to go back. Determined to avoid jail, Blue accelerated to ninety miles per hour, swerving through traffic, and running red lights. The rough-turned sharp curves woke Davon when his head bumped the window.

"What the heck is going on?" Davon yelled as he woke up enough to look behind them.

Trying to focus as much as he could in his impaired state, Blue responded in a panic, "The police are chasing us! I can't go to jail, so I'm gonna out run 'em!"

"Blue, I think I know how to lose them. When we get to Washington Street, take a quick right and cut down through Sheridan Street."

With no response, Blue gripped the steering wheel and stared at the roadway as though entranced. Seconds later, at Washington Street, Blue ran straight through the red light, and he had no time to even think as he saw another car in the intersection.

Traveling straight across Washington Street was a black Kia. The two cars collided in a loud screeching bang that left both Blue and Davon unconscious. The occupants of the Kia were pinned in the mangled wreckage. Bystanders called for police, and within minutes, the area was swarming with police cars, ambulances, and a fire truck.

Blue and Davon were awakened by paramedics. Their faces, clothes, and even the car seats were covered in blood. The driver of the Kia was bruised and bleeding, but she was conscious and able to speak. The passenger of the car, was unresponsive to the tactics of the first responders. She showed no signs of life as the paramedics attempted to revive her. The police worked to control the crowd that gathered around the accident scene and to steer traffic as best they could.

After a few minutes of revival attempts, the Kia passenger was pronounced dead at the scene. Spread out in the backseat of the crushed Kia were a couple of pieces of luggage that had been tossed around. The impact of the crash was so powerful that it tore open the bags, revealing shorts, jeans, colored t-shirts, and one pink bejeweled tank top.

The officer in charge talked to the driver of the Kia, while a second officer went through the purse of the deceased passenger. Tearful, the driver revealed that her name was Vanessa Arnold, and her deceased friend was Kari Brooks.

As the paramedics were rolling Kari's body into the ambulance, and escorting Blue and Davon into the backseat of separate patrol cars, all of the police officers looked at each other and shook their heads. Calls would have to be made to the parents of both girls. The police officers always dreaded this part of the job. More than anything, they dreaded the call they would have to make to Kari Brooks' mother.

Discussion Questions

(Discuss your thoughts with an adult or peer mentor.)

1. How could this accident have been avoided?

2. What do you think Blue and Davon's punishment should be?

3. Have you ever done anything that affected someone else in a negative way? Did you learn anything from that situation? If so, what did you learn?

4. Define "fatal" mistake. Use an event from your local news or online as an example.

5. When Blue and Davon finally realize what happened to Kari, they will know the serious consequences of a stupid decision. How can you avoid making a fatal mistake that could either cost someone their life or devastation that lasts a lifetime?

Chapter Six

Meet me after school

Kim Duncan had been almost stalking Justin Bridges for the past month. The Valentine's Dance was coming up soon, and she wanted someone to invite her. She didn't want to be one of those girls who didn't get an invitation. Besides, she knew she was one of the prettiest girls in school, and she didn't understand why she hadn't been asked to the dance already.

What bothered her most of all was that she had a crush on Justin and he seemed to be looking everywhere but in her direction, and now she was determined to get her crush to ask her to the dance. Justin had liked her in the 6th grade, but back then, she'd had her heart set on Keith Reid. She and Keith had talked a few times, but nothing ever came of it. Now that they were older, and Justin had a few muscles, and a sense of style, Kim thought it was worth her time to take a second look at Justin, and she liked what she saw.

From where she stood, she could see him, leaning against his locker, talking to a few of the boys from his gym class, Justin looked like pure gold to Kim. He was tall for his age, with the deepest dimples to go along with the cutest smile a girl could ask for. The fact that he had been building his muscle tone in the gym didn't hurt him, either.

"What's up, Justin?" Kim wiggled her way between the boys. Being a cheerleader gave Kim a lot of confidence and it showed.

"Hey, Kim," Justin said, dryly. Once upon a time, Justin would have given anything for Kim to even look in his direction, but that was two years ago. Things had changed. He had changed, and he wasn't interested in being Kim's boyfriend anymore.

After a few awkward glances, Justin finally said, "What's up Kim? How can we help you?"

"Justin, can I talk to you alone?" Kim looked around at the other guys, her eyes sending a clear message.

Although he hesitated, Justin said, "Okay." Nodding to his friends, he muttered, "I'll catch up with you guys later."

Once alone at his locker, Kim cozied up to Justin, trying to make small talk while batting her eyelashes. Finally, the subject of the dance came up, and Justin turned away and rolled his eyes. He knew she'd had a reason for coming up to him.

"It will be a lot of fun, Justin, if you go with me." She waited a beat, just to see what he would say, but when he said nothing, she made her intentions clear. "We can have a lot of fun together. Way more than the rest of these silly girls. If you just get to know me better, I'll make it worth your time." Kim had a serious look on her face and no longer was she fluttering her eyelids like an innocent little girl, but she stood in front of Justin, eyes wide open, like a grown woman and waited for his answer.

"Okay, Kim. I hear what you're saying, but I've got someone else that I'm taking to the dance." He didn't want to hurt her feelings by saying what he really wanted to say which was, Giraffes will fly before I will take you to anything.

"Who?" Kim demanded. It felt as though all the wind had been sucked out of her lungs.

"Why, Kim?" Justin asked rhetorically. He really didn't care to hear why she wanted to know. He wasn't going to tell her. If she wanted to know, she would have to go to the dance to find out.

"Well ..."

"Kim, a lot of guys would love to go with you. Why don't you ask one of them, or better yet, let them ask you."

"I'm going with you." With an unsure smile, Kim moved in to grab Justin's arm.

She was too close, and the gesture was too intimate, besides, they were in the school hall and Justin didn't want to be a part of the kind of gossip Kim was trying to start. He sidestepped her until he could back away and head to his next class with his friends.

Kim scowled as she saw Justin's gym buddies looking back at her as they walked away with him undoubtedly asking him questions about what had just happened.

Hurt and rejected, Kim stormed off to her next period class. The closer she got to

34

class, the more her anger subsided. Her next class was English, with Brad Collins. He was not as good looking as Justin, but he would do. She was now determined to get a date to the dance with Brad.

****

The end of the day came fast. Kim had been successful at getting Brad to ask her to the dance because he came outside to join a group of boys and bragged about now much fun he was going to have after the dance with Kim. One of the boys, Gabe Sloan, teasingly asked Brad if she was going to be his girlfriend.

"Are you crazy?" Brad almost shouted. He caught himself and lowered his voice when he saw Kim waving to him from the top of the stairs. "That will never happen. She said we'd have a good time, and I'm trying to have a good time. You know what I mean?"

Gabe cocked his head to the side and snickered. "Yeah, I know what you mean."

Overhearing the entire conversation, Justin knew that Kim had approached Brad because he had turned her down. He silently shook his head at the boys who were high-fiving Brad, and making inappropriate jokes.

Even though Justin was not interested in Kim, he didn't want Brad to take advantage of her. He knew Brad's track record with girls, and a lot of them got more than they wanted with him. Justin didn't want Kim to be one of those girls. She might already know what she's getting herself into, Justin thought. But, if she didn't know, Justin didn't want anything bad to happen to her. After a mini-war in his head about what to do, he decided to warn Kim about Brad. She had to at least go into this date with her eyes open. After that, he'd wash his hands of the whole thing.

****

After homeroom the next day, the roles had been reversed. This time it was Justin looking for Kim. Usually, she would have sashayed by him ten times already to get his attention, but this particular morning, she was nowhere in sight, so he was unrelenting in his search for her.

He spent all of first and second period thinking about Kim. He had almost become obsessed with warning her about Brad's intentions. Justin's knowledge and concerns distracted him so that after his bathroom break, he left the bathroom with toilet tissue stuck to the bottom of his shoe.

In the hallway, a chorus of laughter erupted, and Justin was puzzled as to what was going on. Looking from face to face, he had no clue, until he saw people pointing at the trailing tissue on the bottom of his shoe. Embarrassed, he used the toe of his other shoe to remove the paper. Still uncomfortable, Justin looked up just in time to see Kim looking at him. She was not smiling or laughing like the other kids. Standing across the hall from him, she let her eyes meet Justin's, and her lips tightened into a thin line, before she turned and walked away.

Justin ran to catch up with her, but Mr. Mills, a social studies teacher, stopped him to deliver a mini-lecture about the dangers of running in the halls.

Once Justin was finally free from Mr. Mills, he continued his search for Kim. She was hard to find in the sea of students, but he finally caught sight of her as she ducked into her history class, and he hurried to follow her through the door.

Kim was only a few steps ahead of him, and he reached to touch her shoulder, but she barely spared him a glance. Before he could say a word, Justin saw the teacher, Ms. Morgan, looking at him. She raised her eyebrows in question of his presence in her classroom.

He heard the lie come out of his mouth before he even knew he was going to say it. "Principal Winters wants to see Kim." Justin tried to use his straightest and most innocent face. Ms. Morgan was a young, inexperienced teacher, so he figured he could get away with his lie.

"Okay, Justin," Ms. Morgan didn't question Justin. After all, when she had dropped her bag and all of her papers the day before, Justin had been the only person to help her. The other students just stepped over them.

The teacher may have been deceived by Justin's quick story, but Kim wasn't. She knew he was lying, but instead of causing a scene, Kim stood and left the classroom with Justin.

Once they were out of earshot, Justin had a totally different demeanor than he had the day before when he and Kim had spoken. He seemed to actually care about her, and he wasted no time getting to the point. "Look, I heard you're going to the dance with Brad."

"Yeah, so what?" Kim looked away, staring at the gray lockers lining the walls around them, the tiles on the floor, anywhere other than Justin's face.

"Well, I don't know if you know this or not, but he's got a bad rep with girls."

"So what?"

"What it is is that you might be in over your head. Brad has been known to get what he wants and then he leaves girls alone. Like he doesn't even know them."

"He's not going to do me like that. He treats trashy girls like that." Kim looked Justin in the eyes. After a bit of a stare down, Kim finished the conversation. "Look, I know Brad. He's not going to make me do anything I don't want to."

Kim scowled at Justin as he took one last look at Kim. He regretted that he had even said anything to her. He left her standing in the hall and headed to his math class. He barely missed the tardy bell.

In class, sitting behind him, were three girls. All best friends, Cari, Monica, and Jorden. He could tell something was wrong with Jorden because he could hear her crying and the others trying to console her. While the teacher was distracted with helping a few students with their homework, he listened in on the girls' conversation.

"Girl, it's going to be alright. What did the doctor say?" Cari asked.

Jorden whispered, "He said I have an STD. He said it's permanent." She choked on her words and couldn't say anymore, but Justin couldn't believe what he was hearing. He'd heard about STDs in Health class, but never knew anyone with one.

"What are you going to tell Brad?" Monica wanted to know. "I mean, he should know that he gave you a permanent disease," she continued.

Immediately, Justin knew Monica was talking about Brad Collins because Brad had just bragged in the lunch line about going out with Jorden. Justin reflected on his conversation with Kim, and knew there was absolutely no way she knew this dangerous information about Brad. At that moment, he knew for a fact that there was no possible way that she knew what she was really getting herself into.

Discussion Questions

(Discuss your thoughts with an adult or peer mentor.)

1. Why do you think Kim will do anything just to have a boyfriend?

2. Do you think Justin should tell Kim the new information he's found out? Why or why not?

3. Do you believe Kim has high self-esteem? Why or why not?

4. Do you think Justin should confront Brad about his date with Kim? Why or why not?

5. Do you think Kim is putting herself in a dangerous position? Why or why not?

6. What would you do if you were in Justin's position?

7. What would you do if you were in Kim's position?

8. What would you need to know before trusting someone enough to go out with them?

Chapter Seven

This is Me!

Once you have found all of the words in the word search, use each of the words in sentences to express how they relate to you now, or will relate to you in the future.

```
G U P U C Y E L A R A E V H E
R N S O F B U T I Q V B O S V
E X I Y L F L A A I L N L L I
V U N D P I F D T M O N U A T
E G D L N O T A R R M Z N O A
I D E E Z A R E A H W A T G I
H H U H X E T B N I C E E J C
C L P O P C L S P J X G E T E
A C T O R E E H R K R D R U R
A Y O E H P S L R E W W G N P
M C S P E C I A L A D I Z I P
S U P P O R T I V E V N G Q A
G N I V O L H B X I N S U U J
L U F R E E H C N T G T T E F
M I V O Z T F G R A P C D X M
```

ACHEIVER	APPRECIATIVE
CHEERFUL	COOPERATIVE
EXCELLENT	FAIR
GIVING	HONORABLE
HELPFUL	GOALS

LOVING   NICE

POLITE   PROUD

SPECIAL   SUPPORTIVE

TEAMMATE   UNDERSTANDING

UNIQUE   VOLUNTEER

_____

_____

_____

_____

_____

_____

_____

_____

_____

_____

_____

_____

_____

_____

_____

_____

_____

_____

_____

_____

Chapter Eight

Unlikely Hero

Mrs. Calhoun worked at the front of the room, trying to write math problems on the board, while two students threw paper at each other. Three students walked back and forth across the classroom, visiting other students. The rest of the class was just disinterested, sitting with either their heads down on their desks, or turned around talking to classmates. To a visitor, the classroom scene would have been horrifying, if they didn't know that this was their normal daily routine.

It was March, and somewhere back around October, Mrs. Calhoun had stopped trying to make students listen to her. Now, she was in survival mode, just hoping that if she kept throwing word problems on the wall, someone would catch on and learn something one day. So far, she was wrong.

Her teaching method didn't work and never would. None of the students, not even the good ones, paid her any attention, and instead of learning, Mrs. Calhoun's math class was a free period, as far as the students were concerned. Carlos Martinez was the leader, walking around the room, talking and teasing Mrs. Calhoun. The other students were going about their usual chaotic day, when all of a sudden, a new student walked in, dressed in all black with a blue bandana tied around his head, and another one tucked in the right pocket of his jeans.

Walking into the classroom as though he had already been assigned a seat, the new boy headed straight to the back of the class. He seemed disinterested in anything going on around him, and had no intention of respecting Mrs. Calhoun. Without a word, he slid into a seat, in spite of the fact that someone's book bag was already on top of a desk. Uncaring, the new kid shoved the book bag to the floor.

"Hey dude, that's my stuff!" Carlos Martinez yelled to the back of the room. Carlos had been one of the students out of his seat. He was the class bully, so he felt that he definitely couldn't let this new kid punk him out.

"So what?" The new kid snapped.

"Hey, I said that's my stuff!" Carlos moved closer to the new kid.

"And I said, so what," the kid snapped back, looking out of the window.

Sensing that the new kid might be a little too much to handle, Carlos became more verbal, in hopes of not having to become physical. "Just watch it man. You can't go around slinging people's things around. That's all I'm saying."

Pretending that it was no big deal, Carlos walked back toward the desk of the girl he had been talking to. None of the other students seemed to think that the altercation was a big deal either, as they continued to do what they were doing.

"Excuse me," Mrs. Calhoun addressed the new guy. "Are you Blaze Sullivan?"

"Yeah, why?"

"Young man, please come to the front of the room to get your textbook and paperwork to take home to your parents," Mrs. Calhoun requested.

"I don't do textbooks, and I don't have no parents, so you can keep all that." The class exploded with laughter, but when Blaze looked around at all the other kids with fire in his eyes, the laughs quickly died away.

"Well, you need to have a textbook while you're in class, so please take your book." Mrs. Calhoun looked down to write the book number in her grade book, and avoided making eye contact with Blaze. When Blaze didn't budge, she finally held her head high, straightened her dress, and walked across the room, taking the textbook to him.

"Look old lady, I told you I didn't need no textbook!" He slapped the book from the teacher's hands, and looked Mrs. Calhoun straight in the eye, daring her to challenge him. The students who were yapping it up just a few minutes earlier sat frozen in their seats. Not sure of what else to do, they sat stone still and eerily quiet, waiting for the next move from either Mrs. Calhoun, or Blaze.

"Young man, there is no need to be disrespectful," Mrs. Calhoun tried to take control of the situation.

"I told you there's no need for you to be giving me no book. Get out of my face, lady!" Leaning forward in his seat, Blaze gritted his teeth and stared at Mrs. Calhoun with rage in his eyes.

A look of sheer horror crossed Mrs. Calhoun's face. "I will not tolerate you speaking to me like that." Mrs. Calhoun asserted herself. Her voice may have trembled, but from where the students sat, it was as much from frustration as from fear. They heard the teacher's voice rise, and watched her face. She was so heated that even her glasses started to steam up.

"What I won't tolerate is some teacher telling me what I need and don't need." Blaze's voice was cold and hard. "Matter of fact, I'm out of here." Blaze quickly got up from his chair and pushed past Mrs. Calhoun. He pushed her so hard that she stumbled backward and fell to the floor. Her glasses flew off her face, crashed into a nearby desk, and then hit the tiled floor.

Some of the students felt sorry for Mrs. Calhoun. Probably for the first time that year, they saw her as a frail older lady in distress, instead of the bearer of their boredom. Carlos Martinez was one of the students who felt sorry for Mrs. Calhoun. When it came right down to it, she was just a nice lady trying to do her job.

His feelings were so strong that he intercepted Blaze as he was trying to leave the room. Although a few minutes prior to this incident, it appeared that Carlos was too afraid of Blaze to confront him about throwing his book bag on the floor. Carlos mustered up the courage to speak, "Hey, man, you just knocked over Mrs. Calhoun. What the heck is wrong with you?" Carlos fired off at Blaze.

"Not you again." Standing nearly a foot taller than Carlos, Blaze almost laughed. This time, Carlos didn't back down. He stood up to Blaze. Not blinking, both boys had just began a long stare down when, from the floor, Mrs. Calhoun told the students to call security to her room. One girl ran to the phone and another ran out of the classroom door, in search of an administrator, or the school resource officer.

Mrs. Calhoun, still on the floor, made it apparent that she had hurt something when she fell. She wrinkled her face every time she moved.

"Bring it on punk!" Blaze encouraged Carlos to touch him first. Even Blaze knew that if a person was in a fight, and he had been touched first, he'd get a lighter punishment because he could claim self-defense.

"I'm no punk." Carlos rose up.

"Prove it," Blaze prodded.

Blood rushing to his face, Carlos did the same dance around an imaginary circle that boys do when they don't really want to fight, but feel their manhood is at stake if they don't. He walked in a circle, pumping his fist into the palm of his hand, and Blaze did the same.

Taunting Carlos, Blaze said something about Carlos' mother – that was all the provoking he needed. Carlos leapt onto Blaze like a frog, and began to punch him in the face and neck. Blaze blocked and punched back. After a very hard punch on the lip, Blaze's blood went everywhere. Carlos had busted Blaze's lip.

Enraged, Blaze struggled to pull something out of his pocket. When he finally pulled it free, all the class could see was shiny metal in his hand. He had a very sharp-looking knife. Before Carlos realized what was going on, Blaze lunged at him full speed, with the knife pointed at his head.

Just before Blaze was close enough to penetrate Carlos' skin with the knife, the school police officer, the principal, and the security officer pulled Blaze away. It seemed as if each of the men had a limb, and they were all pulling as if they meant to pull the large boy apart. Blaze ended up on his stomach, and the school police officer quickly pulled Blaze's hands behind his back, and slapped handcuffs on him.

The principal, Mr. Winfrey, ran over to Mrs. Calhoun to assess the situation. When Mr. Winfrey asked Mrs. Calhoun what happened, she told him briefly, but was sure to mention that Carlos had tried to intervene on her behalf, and that she was truly grateful.

After the police and the security guard left with Blaze in tow, all of Mrs. Calhoun's students returned quietly to their desks, speechless after what had just happened in their classroom.

Carlos sat near the front of the classroom with the school nurse examining him. Once she saw that he only had a few visible scratches, she told him to go with her to call his mom. Before he left with the nurse, Mrs. Calhoun motioned for Carlos to come to her. She was still on the floor. Principal Winfrey realized that it was unsafe to move her, so he was calling an ambulance on his cell phone.

"What you did for me was so brave. What made you step in like that?" Mrs. Calhoun's voice was weak.

"I just couldn't sit back and let him push you down like that. We may talk and horseplay, but he took it way too far by putting his hands on you. My mom went through that before, with her ex-boyfriend, and it's just not cool." Everyone was silent for a moment, before Carlos continued, "I just couldn't let him to do that to you."

Discussion Questions

(Discuss your thoughts with an adult or peer mentor.)

1. What do you think should happen to Blaze? Why?

2. Why did Carlos stand up for Mrs. Calhoun even though he had also disrespected her? Why do you think that reason was important to him?

3. What could Carlos have done instead of fighting Blaze?

4. What would you do if you encountered a situation like what happened in Mrs. Calhoun's class?

5. Does having a weapon really help solve problems or create more problems? Why or why not?

6. How could this whole thing have been avoided?

7. Why is being respectful to teachers and other adults important?

Chapter Nine

There's no place like home

Will Wallace pulled the covers over his head and shuddered, as he was awakened from his sleep to shouting. His mom and older brother, Ty, were arguing again. This was the third night in a row that he had awakened in the middle of the night, because his brother came home at two a.m. on a school night. Will didn't have the heart to tell his mom that it really didn't matter how late Ty was coming home, because he wasn't going to school, anyway.

Their mother, Ms. Wallace, was a nurse and most days she had to be at the hospital by six a.m. Will and Ty usually weren't even up when she left for work. She had no idea, most days, what they were even wearing to school, or whether or not they were eating breakfast. Will didn't like that his mom couldn't see him off to school, but he didn't take advantage of it like Ty did.

Ty would skip school, bring girls over to their house, and on a few occasions, Will had seen Ty drink liquor. Their mom didn't keep beer, wine, or any other kind of liquor in the house, so Will didn't know where Ty had gotten the liquor from. From the sound of Ty's voice, this particular evening, he'd probably been drinking again.

The drinking was bad enough, on its own, but Will had seen videos at school, about teenagers who were permanently injured or died due to injuries caused by drinking and driving. Will always cringed when he went to bed and saw his brother wasn't in his bed. He didn't want his brother to be the subject of one of those drunk driving video lessons.

Will wanted to tell Ty how he felt, but since Ty had been going out at night, his personality had drastically changed. He wasn't the easygoing guy he used to be. Now, he liked to argue, criticize, and berate Will. Most days, Will tried to just avoid him. Ty was a long way from the brother Will used to love to play football with.

That night, it seemed as if Ty had taken his crazy behavior to another level. Will actually heard his brother saying horrible things to his mom and occasionally he heard something fall, or possibly thrown to the floor. With a steady stream of thuds and loud arguing, it was going to be impossible for Will to go back to sleep, and he worried that his mother or brother would really get hurt.

Rising slowly, Will sat at the edge of the bed. It was as if with sitting up, the arguing got louder and more intense. He wrestled with the thought of going into the living room to intervene. He knew Ty was much larger than him, so his presence would probably do little good. As Will wiped the sleep out of his eyes, he heard a loud thud that seemed to have cracked a wall. A cracking sound immediately followed the thud. Those sounds along with the alarming scream of his mother jolted Will out of the bed. He tripped over shoes left beside his bed, managed to find his footing, and sprinted into the family room to see what had happened.

In the family room, he saw his mom on the floor with blood on her face, in her hair, and on her shirt and hands. Ty was standing there looking down at her. Angry, he breathed hard through flared nostrils. If he weren't human, Will could have sworn his brother was breathing fire. Ty's hands were fisted and he seemed to be contemplating beating his mother again.

Heartbroken, Will couldn't just stand there and wait to see what Ty was going to do. He ran across the room like he was running a fifty yard dash and tackled Ty, taking him down like a football linebacker.

Ty tried to punch Will, but Will's rage made him much stronger than Ty, even though he was much smaller than him. Ty's drinking impaired him just enough for Will to get the upper hand. Will was able to grab Ty's hands and put a grip on him that eventually tired Ty out, so that he stopped fighting. Exhausted, he even seemed to sober up a bit.

While Will had Ty pinned down, their mother was able to pick herself up from the floor and limp over to the phone to call the police. The police must have been in the neighborhood already because it only took them a few minutes to ring the doorbell.

After relieving Will of his restraining duties, two policemen handcuffed Ty, and while one officer took Ty outside to talk to him, the other spoke to Will and his mother.

The police took a few pictures of Will's mom's injuries, and then placed Ty in the back of the squad car and pulled out of their driveway, leaving Will and his mom sitting on the sofa not saying a word, silent tears running down both their faces. Finally, Will's mom stood up and straightened her nightgown and said, "I've got to be up in two hours, and you've got school tomorrow. Let's try to get some sleep."

Understanding his mom's need to not talk about what had just happened, Will followed his mom down the hallway, and when she turned to go into her bedroom, he turned to go to his. Before closing his door, he looked over at her door to see if she had lingered there to give a hug, or one final word before closing herself off from him, but she had already closed the door.

****

A very long month passed, and although Ty was still away from home, he wasn't in an adult jail. Will's mom had given permission for Ty to go to a detention program out of town. It was detention camp for boys like him who were dealing with destructive behavioral patterns.

This camp placed the fear of going to jail in so-called, "bad boys." The officers made their time there a living nightmare. They had to wake up at 4 a.m. every morning to do fifty pushups. After that, they ran twenty laps around the camp and repeated this workout until either someone threw up or passed out. Then, they would do some labor like picking up trash all day or digging trenches to turn around and fill them back in.

Home alone, on a rainy night, Will couldn't help feeling a bit abandoned. Back before Ty became, "Terrible Ty," he and Will would tell ghost stories on a gloomy, rainy night. As morbid as ghost stories could be, sitting with his brother, sharing the scary fun always lifted Will's spirits. This particular night, nothing seemed to lift Will's spirits. His brother was gone, his mom was working, and he felt so alone. The ring of the telephone snapped Will out of his pity party, enough for him to answer the phone and put it on speakerphone.

"Hello?"

"Hey, man!" Ty's energetic voice was on the other end, clearly glad to have reached someone.

"What's up?" Will perked up. "Is this really you?" Feeling stupid for even asking the question, but after a month of not talking to his brother, Will was starting to feel like he might never talk to him again.

"Are you still at that camp?" Will wanted to know.

"Yeah, I'm still here, but I'm leaving in a week."

"For real?" Will asked incredulously, "Where are you going?"

"Home, bro'. I'm coming home."

Will felt his heart pound so hard that he could almost hear the sound of it. He couldn't believe that his brother was coming home – finally. But as happy as the news made him, he had mixed feelings: what if Ty hadn't changed? What if he'd gotten worse? What if he couldn't change? But deep in his heart, more than anything, Will wanted the brother he loved and trusted back in his life.

"So, why are they letting you come home so soon? I thought the program was supposed to last two months."

"They said they think I've learned my lesson. It normally takes people longer, but I learned my lesson after about two weeks."

"It's been a month, Ty. You've been gone a whole month ..."

"Sounds like you've been counting the days, bro'." Ty chuckled and paused before he continued on a more serious note, "Will, you don't ever want to come here. I've seen some things in here that I promise, had me sleepless and in tears." Ty said that part a little quieter than everything else. He didn't want everyone to know he had been crying. Will was quiet stunned by his brother's honesty.

"Alright, well, just tell Mama I need her to pick me up next Monday. She can call here to get the rest of the info." Ty paused again, then asked, "Is she home?"

"Nope."

"Alright, well, I'll see you when I get home." It was quiet for a minute and then Ty added, "Things will be different, Will. I apologize for what I put you guys through. I had to learn the hard way, in here. I'm not trying to be locked up for the rest of my life like an animal, not being able to do anything or go anywhere. In here, everybody looks at you like you're doing something wrong, even when you're not. That's not what I want out of life." Ty took a deep breath. "I've seen some kids in here whose parents are dead, and they had to live on the streets, or their parents don't care what they're doing. Mama's always been there for us. She works so hard to get us what we need. She didn't deserve what I did. Tell Mama I said I'm sorry."

Wondering why his brother wouldn't or couldn't tell their mother how he was feeling, Will listened to his brother pour his heart out. Just as he heard Ty tell someone that he would be off the phone in a second, their mother walked into the room. Hearing the floor creak behind him, Will looked over his shoulder and saw his mother standing there, smiling. She had overheard most of the conversation.

"Hello? Will? Are you still there?" Ty questioned. Will had become silent once he saw his mother.

"Yeah," Will said slowly as his mother walked closer and laid a hand on his shoulder.

Leaning closer to the phone, giving her younger son's shoulder a squeeze, Ms. Wallace clearly had something to say, and Will took a step back from the phone. "I'm here, Ty, and I know. I love you, Son." Their mother had overheard the most important part of the conversation from the speakerphone.

"Mom, I'm sorry for all I put you and Will through. I've learned my lesson. Can I come home?"

Without hesitation, Ms. Wallace said, "Yes, Ty. We want you to come home."

"Thank you, Mama. It's going to be different. I promise you that. I'm not coming back here. I will never disappoint you again."

"Okay, Baby, I believe you. We'll see you soon." Ms. Wallace responded with a smile.

After everyone said their goodbyes, Will hung up the phone. He and Ms. Wallace sat in silence until Will broke the stillness of the room.

"I hope he's right Mom ... I hope he's right."

Discussion Questions

(Discuss your thoughts with an adult or peer mentor.)

1. Why do you think it took Ty going to the detention camp to realize he was wrong?

2. Why do you think he took his mother for granted?

3. Ty realized that he put Will and his mother through a lot. Do you think he has learned his lesson this time? Why or why not? Give evidence.

4. How would you feel if Will's family situation happened to you? What would you do?

5. Why is it important to show respect to your parents or guardians?

6. What kinds of things played into the choices that Ty decided to make?

7. How did those choices affect his family?

8. What kind of an example did Ty set for his younger brother, Will?

9. Does Ty have an obligation to be a role model for Will? Why?

10. Does Ty have an obligation to his mother? If so, what is it?

Chapter Ten

Lunch Money

"Come on Dane, I've had to give you my lunch money every day for the last two weeks. My mom doesn't get home until late, so I don't get to eat after breakfast. Please, don't take my money today. I need to eat!"

Dane Monroe sneered at Matthew Rowland as Matthew continued emptying his pockets. "For real, Dane, if you keep doing this, I'm gonna …"

"You're going to what?" Dane interjected, daring him to say he'd tell someone.

More humbled, Matthew started again. "It's just that I'm hungry, and I need to eat."

"If you don't give me your money, you're not going to want to eat. You won't have any teeth to eat with." Dane and his posse of four other boys roared with laughter at his comeback. Dane stood almost six feet tall with broad shoulders and a muscular build. Matthew was four inches over five feet, with a slim build. Dane was definitely too big to be picking on Matthew.

"So, when are you gonna stop taking my money?" Matthew asked with a glimmer of hope that the madness might end soon.

"I won't ever stop taking your money." Dane pushed Matthew to the ground, and high-fived an almost six foot tall buddy. The buddy had a little more fear in his eyes than Dane did. It was easy to tell that if Dane hadn't coerced the guy, along with the others in his posse, he probably wouldn't be in his group of bandits. Dejected, Matthew looked down into the dirt with an angry scowl on his face.

Dane continued, "Look, just come out here tomorrow at the same time, and maybe, just maybe …" Matthew perked up. He believed Dane was going to say he would stop harassing him. Dane continued, 'Maybe I'll let you keep your teeth." The group howled again as Dane took the last bit of change along with a few dollar bills out of Matthew's pockets.

Matthew had thought about hiding his money somewhere else, but he could only imagine the beating would be worse if Dane expected to get his money and Matthew didn't have any.

After the posse moved on to harass another boy, Matthew picked himself up from the ground and dusted himself off. He had been prepared to fight for his money today, but after Dane knocked him on the ground, his heroic idea quickly faded. He thought pleading for his money might help, but it didn't.

On his way home, Matthew passed a lot of thrift stores, grocery stores, and pawn shops. One place he passed stood out to him, on this particular day. He hadn't noticed it before, and he didn't know how long it had been there, but right at the corner of Fifth and Washington Streets, was Harry's Boxing and Tae Kwon Do Gym.

Matthew hadn't seen this place before, but by the looks of it, it hadn't been there too long. There was a young man, probably not much older than Matthew, standing out-side of the gym, passing out flyers. The boy handed Matthew a flyer, and he looked at it suspiciously. When he saw the monthly cost of twenty dollars, he threw the flyer into the nearest trashcan. No sooner had he thrown it away, than a short, muscular man came out to the street and approached Matthew.

"So, you don't think this is for you, huh?" The man looked past Matthew, but spoke to him at the same time.

"Huh?" Matthew was puzzled as to why the man was even speaking to him.

"You threw the flyer away. To me, it looks like you're one of the main little guys around here who needs it."

"What?" A stunned and insulted Matthew questioned.

"That's the same thing I say every day when I see you let that fella take your money." Now, the imposing stranger was looking directly at Matthew.

"Look, I'm okay. I guess Dane is just in a little money crunch right now. It won't be like this next week." Matthew was hoping that saying it aloud would make it true, but deep down, he was afraid it wouldn't be true for a very long time.

"Alright young man. If you say so. My name's Harry. You come on back if that boy keeps messing with you. We'll show you what to do with him!" The man turned and walked back towards the building and disappeared inside.

The next day at school, Dane walked down the hall, and bumped Matthew's shoulders. "Punk, meet me by the steps at 11:00, and don't forget my money."

Dane put emphasis on his wicked greeting by ramming his right fist into his open left palm. He and his boys rounded the corner, their laughter following them. Matthew looked down into his pocket, saw his lunch money, and heard his empty stomach growl. It was then that he decided that he didn't have much to lose by going to Harry's.

When Matthew walked inside the gym after school, it was a totally different world. Boys and men were hitting punching bags, jumping rope, sparing, running laps on the indoor track, and lifting weights. He even saw kids his age sparring like pros. That caught his eye. He figured if he could learn how to do that, Dane would leave him alone for good.

Harry came out of nowhere, just as he had the day before, and walked up behind Matthew. "I knew you'd come back, he said, pulling his sparring gloves on his hands. "How'd you know that?" Matthew asked, still trying to figure out why Harry even cared about his situation.

"I just know," Harry said smugly.

"Well, can you help me?"

"I can help you if you help yourself. You're off to a good start though. Coming here was a good first step," Harry responded.

"What do we start with? Can I have some gloves?"

"Whoa, slow down some. We need to condition you first."

"Okay. As long as you can get me in shape enough to whip Dane, I'll be good."

"I'm going to teach you that, but I'm also going to teach you to have the power to not have to resort to fighting."

"What? How are you going to teach me not to fight? Isn't fighting what the whole gym is all about?"

"This gym is about a lot more than fighting. It's about getting something in you that makes people respect you, and makes you respect yourself."

"That's all good and everything, but I thought you saw what was going on every day with Dane. I need to know how to fight a dude who's bigger than me. Now, can you help me do that or not?"

"I can help you do that, but it doesn't come free."

"Aw, man! I don't have any money to pay you. First Dane, now you. Everybody's trying to get money out of me. I knew there had to be a catch," Matthew couldn't hide his disappointment.

"You don't have to pay me with money. You pay me with knowledge."

"Huh?" Matthew looked puzzled.

"I'm going to teach you how to fight, but I'm also going to teach you everything I know about making this guy get off your back with non-physical communication. That's verbal, mental, and spatial. And, then if that doesn't work, you have my permission to unleash the beast on him. Okay?"

Matthew didn't really understand everything Harry was talking about, but he did put together that Harry wanted him to talk to Dane first, and if that didn't work, he could fight him. Matthew would do anything to get to the learning how to fight part, so he agreed. The two shook hands, and then Harry made Matthew run so many laps around the track that he almost floated out of his body. Matthew thought he was training for the Olympics rather than a school yard fight. When he was finished, Matthew collapsed on the floor beside Harry and breathlessly asked, "What does this have to do with fighting or even talking to Dane like you want me to?"

"Running is always good for the soul. Plus, I needed to see how serious you were. The fact that you didn't stop after the first ten laps proved to me you were in it for the long haul. Be here tomorrow right after school. That's all for today."

Matthew was feeling a little irritated that Harry had basically tricked him, but he could also see where Harry was coming from once he had cooled down. Leaving the gym, Matthew felt something that he hadn't felt in a long time. Hope.

****

Matthew continued to train at Harry's every day for the next week, and each day, Dane took Matthew's money right before lunch. Right in the middle of Matthew's second week of training, something happened to him. He felt power! Harry had been teaching him to have word fights. In that type of skirmish, you have to outwit your opponent by outthinking them and using their own words to keep them off-balance. Harry had also been teaching him the game of chess which was another way Matthew was learning to outsmart his opponent. In the thought fights, a person had to think themselves superior to the other person. It was almost like reverse psychology except with the sparring techniques Matthew was learning at Harry's he could actually back up his thought fights with a physical fight if necessary.

A month or so into his training at Harry's, Matthew had a chance to test his new abilities. Matthew hadn't asked Harry if he thought he was ready or not to use his skills, he just felt ready. Besides, he was tired of being pushed around, and after a few minutes of Dane's usual threats, Matthew looked him in the eyes and asked, "So, what is it that you want from me?"

"What are you talking about?" Dane laughed and looked away. Harry had prepared Matthew for Dane's looking away. Harry taught Matthew to maintain eye contact by any means necessary. Harry taught him that looking into the eyes of someone was a must. Many attackers can't stand to see their victims in a human light, and looking into their victim's eyes couldn't make them any more human.

Matthew made sure to maintain eye contact. "What do you really want from me? There are hundreds of kids at this school that you could get money from, but day after day, you choose to pick me to harass. Why? What is it that you really want from me?" Matthew still held eye contact.

"Man, you're crazy. I don't want nothing from you, other than your money," he laughed.

Matthew gave Dane something called an accountability stare. It was a mean stare mixed with the idea of, I'm holding you accountable for what you do to me. Dane had never seen these looks, nor had he heard this talk from Matthew before. He saw a different side of him. He saw confidence and a refusal to be beaten down. Dane saw that Matthew was not the same guy he had been intimidating for weeks. He saw that Matthew was not willing to be a victim, and he wasn't going to be easily controlled.

Finally, Matthew warned Dane, "If I have to fight today, I will do it."

56

"You're gonna have to fight all of us." Dane reminded him.

"Bring it on."

The serious look on his face told Dane that Matthew felt strong and sure of himself. Matthew wasn't weak or easy, and that made Dane take a step back. Looking back at his crew, Dane made a decision. "You're not worth it," he finally said, walking away.

Watching Dane and his crew walk away, Matthew was so busy standing his ground and not letting himself be nervous, he didn't realize how nervous he really was. Once Dane and the crew were out of the way, Matthew's hands began to shake. It was just nervous energy, he knew, but it was also the overwhelming understanding that although he was prepared to fight, he didn't have to. He was no longer a victim, and it felt good to have control over how he was treated. He was proud of himself for standing his ground, and he was grateful to Harry for giving him the confidence to do it.

Discussion Questions

(Discuss your thoughts with an adult or peer mentor.)

1. Do you think that Dane's friends wanted to bully Matthew? If you think they didn't want to, why did they do it?

2. Why do you think that giving Dane "the look," and boldly speaking to him made him leave Matthew alone?

3. Why do you think Dane chose to bully Matthew?

4. Have you ever been bullied or have you been a bully? Explain and answer honestly.

5. What makes a person a target for a bully?

6. In what ways can a person bully another person?

7. How would you feel if you were bullied every day?

8. What should you do if you become a victim of bullying? What should you do if you see a situation of bullying?

9. Why do you think Matthew felt good about the outcome even though he didn't use the fighting skills he had worked so hard to learn?

10. Remember Shena in Chapter Two? What are similarities between Shena's bullying and Dane's bullying? What are the differences?

Chapter Eleven

This is Me, Too!

Once you have found all of the words in the word search, use each of the words in sentences to express how they relate to you now or will relate to you in the future.

```
E E H E O I H S M K E S R R C
N C U V R B N O S R W E X I P
I O M S I E R T E E L N T E A
L C I O Q A S V E I N I N F Y
P A L T L E E P A G Z D L T I
I R I S A S D B E E R E N T X
C I T E R R L T N C S I R I D
S N Y E O E E S N A T O T X K
I G P U G Q H P R Q P S V Y V
D J E L B I S N O P S E R T C
W G Z B P A U T U O I D S S E
C O N T R O L S S B C T Y E T
E N D U R A N C E U T L T N I
X K R O W M A E T Z R S U O Q
S C I H T E U Z H Q W T D H Z
```

CARING   CITIZENSHIP
COOPERATION   DISCIPLINE
DUTY   ENDURANCE
ETHICS   HONESTY
HUMILITY   INTEGRITY
KINDNESS   MORALS
PERSEVERE   RELIABLE
RESPECT   RESPONSIBLE

TRUST   CITIZENSHIP
COOPERATION   DISCIPLINE
DUTY   ENDURANCE
ETHICS   HONESTY
HUMILITY   INTEGRITY
KINDNESS   MORALS
PERSEVERE   RELIABLE
RESPECT   RESPONSIBLE
SUPPORT   TEAMWORK
TRUST

Chapter Twelve

The New Job

Hand in hand, Mr. and Mrs. Belton walked into the house from their date night. It had been months since the two of them had been able to spend some time alone. With Mr. Belton taking a higher paying job across town, date nights were not the only things that had become limited in the Belton household. Now that he was working two additional hours every night, and his commute from work took a little over an hour extra, he almost always missed school events and games.

Before the job change, Lori and Dennard were used to their father always being at every one of their school and recreational functions, and Mrs. Belton was used to having her weekly date night. That was something they had agreed on, way back when they were newlyweds, seventeen years earlier. They never missed a date night until Mr. Belton took that new job, but the family needed the money that came with the inconvenience of Mr. Belton's new work hours.

The family needed more money because Lori was in cheerleading and Dennard was a football player. They both needed a substantial amount of money to participate in their sport. Mrs. Belton was taking up Mrs. Belton's slack around the house and going to all of the kids' school events and games. Not to mention, picking them up from practice every day.

This new job was causing a strain on everyone in the family, but no one more than Mr. Belton. He was often cranky when he did finally make it home, and his once positive attitude had shifted, terribly. There were many days when he felt the extra money just wasn't worth it. But, he didn't want to quit. They needed the money. He felt he'd just have to sacrifice until they could do a little better.

So, this date night was extra special to Mr. and Mrs. Benton. It was a brief relief from all the tension and stress they'd both been facing. When they opened the garage door leading to the kitchen, both Dennard and Lori were in the kitchen raiding the refrigerator.

"Some night out you had," Dennard said sarcastically.

"Yeah, you guys are home really early. Did something happen?" Lori chimed in.

"No, sweetie. Nothing happened. Your dad just has to get up early and go to work tomorrow, so we couldn't stay out too late."

"Work, again?" Dennard asked, shaking his head.

"Yeah, Dad. I thought you were off tomorrow. You know I have my cheerleading competition. This is only the second time Eastview High has ever made it this far; it's kind of a big deal, and you said you'd come," Lori looked her father directly in the eye, hoping that he would say that he'd be able to come.

"I know, honey, but they've had some layoffs in my department, and I have to pick up the slack to make sure things go smoothly on Monday. I'm just fortunate not to be one of the ones who was laid off, especially since I've only been recently hired.

Downcast, Lori looked away and nodded in agreement with her father. She knew he had been blessed to get that job, but since he'd taken it, the whole family had only felt cursed.

"Look, in a few more months, I'll qualify for a raise, and could get promoted. If that happens, I can make some of my own hours and even work from home one day a week. I promise, it won't be this way for long," Mr. Belton explained, hoping that it would give his family some peace.

The family seemed satisfied with his promises and Mrs. Belton and Lori kissed each of his cheeks, and Dennard gave his dad a fist bump, as Mr. Belton headed upstairs to bed.

After Mr. Belton went upstairs, Lori and Dennard vented to their mother about how unfair things seemed to be now that their dad was working at the new job. She agreed, but consoled them, and told them that if they were patient, things would be back to normal in no time. Even though she said those words to her children, Mrs. Belton didn't know if she really believed them herself.

****

One week later, Dennard was sitting in his history class, soaking it up. History was his favorite subject and Mr. Wolfe was an outstanding teacher. Out of all the school subjects he disliked, Dennard actually looked forward to history class each day. The class was breaking into groups for an activity, when Dennard heard his name called over the intercom.

"Come to the principal's office?" Dennard knew he hadn't done anything wrong lately, so he didn't know what he was being called to the office for. When he got to the waiting area outside of the principal's office, Lori was already sitting there. He knew then that something was definitely wrong, because Lori never did anything to be called to the principal's office.

Mr. Walters, the principal, came to the door of his office and motioned for both Dennard and Lori to come in.

Entering, they immediately saw their mom. She had a worried look on her face, but when she saw her children, she immediately tried to smile.

"Mama, what's going on?" Lori blurted out.

"Baby, it's your dad," She paused for a moment to gather herself, and then continued, "He had an accident on the way to work this morning. It looks as though he might have fallen asleep while he was driving."

"Is he okay?" Dennard wanted to know.

"He's in the hospital," Mrs. Belton hesitated to say the rest. "He's in a coma." She choked back tears, because saying it out loud to her children actually made it real.

"How could this happen?" Dennard's eyes had grown wide in disbelief. He didn't know their mother had just told them everything she knew.

"I came to pick you both up, to take you to the hospital to see him. That may help him to come around sooner, if he knows we're all there for him."

"Mama, he is going to be alright, right?" Lori questioned.

"Baby, I pray so. I don't know much right now, but we just have to pray."

****

The ride to the hospital was quiet. Everyone was lost in their own thoughts of what if?

When they entered the hospital room, Mr. Belton was on a ventilator and he was badly bruised. His head had been bandaged, and so had his arms and legs. The sight of her injured father was enough to cause Lori to burst into tears.

The doctor came in wearing his surgery scrubs. "Mrs. Belton, we had to operate. We were able to stop the internal bleeding, and I expect him to recover completely, but he has to wake up."

"We just need him to wake up, then? When will he wake up?" Lori asked tearfully.

"We don't know," The doctor looked at Mr. Belton. "That's going to be on him. Hopefully, with you all here, he'll feel enough love to wake up soon." The doctor used a series of medical terms to explain Mr. Belton's condition. When he was done, the doctor left the family sitting in their small stiff group. Mrs. Belton finally broke their stillness by going over to her husband's bedside and holding his hand. Dennard and Lori followed her, Lori standing on the opposite side of the bed from their mother, and Dennard sat on the side of the bed. Holding hands, they prayed for Mr. Belton to wake up. They each said their own special prayer, cried, and hugged each other. Mr. Belton didn't move or open his eyes, but his family felt comforted, and they felt confident that he would be alright if only he would wake up.

****

It had been two weeks since the accident, and Dennard and Lori still went to school each day, but only to try to get their minds off of their father's condition. It was difficult though. Their bodies were at school, but their minds were worlds away. They would both find themselves distant and unfocused while in class, or with friends.

It was during literature class, when Dennard got the message to go to the principal's office. He felt knots in his stomach. After the family's prayer at the hospital, he had been praying multiple times a day for his dad's recovery. He had felt so confident that day in the hospital that everything would be okay, but now, walking to the principal's office, he felt anything but confident. He felt sick to his stomach. Seeing his sister round the corner, as they both walked into the principal's office together, he could tell she was feeling the same way.

He wanted to be strong for her, but he couldn't deny the fear he felt. In a haze of confusion, he didn't realize he had shed a tear. When he realized it, he quickly wiped it away, but it was too late. Lori had already seen it. Panic erupted on her face. Dennard put his arm around Lori, steadying her as they quickly and quietly walked into the front office. The secretary motioned for them to go straight back to the principal's office. Inside, they found their mom. With her back to them, they couldn't see her facial expression to know whether things were good or bad, and they both felt a shimmer of fear.

"Oh, you're here," the principal stood, when Lori and Dennard took another step into the office.

"Is Dad ..." Lori's cold fingers gripped Dennard's whole hand.

Mrs. Belton turned to them with the biggest smile they'd ever seen on her face, and they knew the news was good. She explained that their father had awakened, and even had a conversation with her. He desperately wanted to see Lori and Dennard.

Relieved, this time when they left the principal's office, the family was crying tears of joy, instead of pain. When they finally reached the hospital, Mr. Belton was sitting up, eating a liquid meal. Lori and Dennard laughed as Dennard yelled, "Dad's back! Hide all the food!" All four of them laughed and even the nurse chuckled.

The Belton family continued laughing and joking around with each other and it felt like old times again. When Mr. Belton started getting tired, Mrs. Belton suggested that it was time to take Lori and Dennard home. Before they left, Mr. Belton gathered his family around his bedside and said, "I know you all have been really scared the last few weeks. I don't know what the future holds. There are a lot of things we can't control, but there are also a lot of things we can control. I promise you that from here on out, I will be there for you all, if it's humanly within my power. I'm resigning from my job and I'm going to take my old job back, if they will have me. No amount of money is worth not being here with you."

Mrs. Belton hugged her husband, being careful not to hurt his bruised body. Dennard and Lori looked at each other and smiled. They knew they'd have their supportive dad back. After a long while of visiting, they left the room feeling closer as a family because they had weathered the storm and now they were seeing the rainbow. They all realized that nothing could replace family.

Discussion Questions

(Discuss your thoughts with an adult or peer mentor.)

1. Have you ever had to deal with a family crisis? Did it bring your family together or tear them apart? Why or why not?

2. Do you think this family will be a lot more appreciative of each other as a result of the accident? Why or why not?

3. What are some ways you might deal with family illness or tragedy in a positive way?

4. How can you help someone who has had to deal with illness or tragedy?

5. What lesson can we learn from this story about families overcoming adversity?

Topic: Kindness

Chapter Thirteen

Azilee who?

Birch Street was quiet, unbelievably so. It was five o'clock in the evening and all the kids on the block were in their homes. This wasn't strange, because with the weather being in the teens and low twenties lately, it was too cold to play outside. Atlanta wasn't used to this kind of weather, so all of the kids spent their time inside playing video games, watching television, online, or texting. Alicia was no different.

She was sitting in her house watching television. Her house was nestled midway down the street; not much happened on Alicia's street without her knowing about it. So, when she heard the loud siren so close to her home, she knew something bad was happening. She rushed to her window to look out.

Alicia was accustomed to hearing sirens, but usually they were in the distance. This one sounded like it was at the front door. As she rushed over to the window, her mother bolted in from the kitchen. They were both in a frenzy, thinking that one of their neighbors might be in trouble.v

Looking out of the window, they noticed that the ambulance or fire truck was not on their street. This puzzled them, so in an attempt to investigate, they went outside to see if they could find the source of the sirens and where they were going. As soon as they stepped outside, they realized that the sirens were not on their street, but the next street over. The smell and fog of suffocating smoke came from the house directly behind theirs. It was Azilee's Hooper's home that was on fire, and from the looks of it, there was more fire than house left.

Azilee Hooper had moved to their neighborhood six months, earlier. She came from a small country town in South Georgia. All the kids at school made fun of her country accent and her country way of dressing. Even her hairstyles were the source of many jokes on the bus ride to and from school, and it was the cause of many classroom disruptions.

One day at school, Alicia was trying to decide on a hairstyle to wear to her friend's birthday party. Azilee overheard her, and trying to be helpful and friendly, Azilee said, "You can borrow this hair magazine. I just got it in the mail."

Looking back, she had to have had a lot of courage to even speak to Alicia, being that Alicia was one of the most popular girls at the school. Instead of considering Azilee's courage to even say something, Alicia had quickly looked at Azilee's hairdo and said, "No thank you."

Alicia wasn't really trying to be mean or funny, but all the kids in her class thought it was the funniest thing that had been said all year, so they erupted with laughter. They laughed for at least ten minutes and they even carried the joke over into lunch time.

Kevin Giddons was the instigator. He just wouldn't leave it alone. The rest of Azilee's day was miserable because of it. Alicia could see it on her face; and it was all because Azilee had tried to be helpful to Alicia. Even after that day, Kevin continued to tease Azilee about her hair and clothes. Since that day, Azilee never again tried to talk to Alicia. Alicia had once thought about apologizing to Azilee in the hallway because she'd felt so bad about everything, but when Alicia's friends came by, Alicia joined in with them and Azilee wouldn't even look at her.

Now, as Alicia stood watching the remains of Azilee's house go up in flames, she knew that Azilee could use a friend, but probably wouldn't even want to see her. Matter of fact, Alicia thought, she didn't see Azilee and her family standing outside. Could they all still be inside the house, strangled by the same smoke that had assaulted her and her mom?

Alicia began to panic and asked her mom what to do. They began asking neighbors if they'd seen the family pull into the garage. It was too hot to touch the garage door to see if their car was in there. Two minutes later, everyone would be able to see the answer to their question, because as the firefighters were working on saving the home, the garage burned to the ground. No car was in sight.

As soon as firefighters had the burn under control, Azilee's family's blue mini-van pulled up on the street. Policemen stopped them from getting near the house, as they had all the other cars. Mr. and Mrs. Hooper ran over to the police line which is as close to the remains of the haouse as anyone could go, and as they watched their home go up in smoke, Azilee, her little brother, and little sister came to stand beside them. Mrs. Hooper began to cry and that made Azilee and her sister and brother cry. Biting his bottom lip, Mr. Hooper tried to console them, as he visibly fought back his own tears.

All of the neighbors went up to the family and offered their assistance. Many not truly wanting the inconvenience of taking in a family of five, but it just seemed like the right thing to do. Alicia and her mom were among the few neighbors offering genuine help.

Mr. and Mrs. Hooper graciously thanked everyone for their kind words and thoughts, but there was a look of overwhelming confusion and pain on their faces. Six months earlier, they had moved to this neighborhood in an effort to build something good for their family, and now they were faced with having to start over again. They were rightfully overwhelmed. As Alicia's mom spoke to Azilee's parents, Alicia took the time to speak to Azilee. With tears in her eyes, Azilee looked at Alicia with wordless pain.

"Azilee, I'm so sorry this happened to you all. I will do whatever I can to help, if you don't mind."

"Mind?" Azilee looked at the remains of her home, then back at her neighbor. "I … I don't mind," she whispered.

Feeling bad, Alicia nodded. She wanted to help, but she also wanted to apologize for that day in school three months ago, when she caused the entire class to laugh at Azilee's hair and clothes, but it just felt wrong bringing that up at a time like this. Alicia was sure that hair had to be the last thing on Azilee's mind. After saying their goodbyes, Alicia and her mom headed home.

Alicia was determined to make good on her promise to Azilee. She couldn't imagine losing everything in her home to a fire. Even though no one liked Azilee's clothes or shoes, they were hers and it had to hurt to lose them.

As soon as Alicia walked into her house, it was as though a light bulb went off in her head, just like on the cartoons. She remembered something her pastor said the previous Sunday. He had said, "Sometimes, God will use a tragedy to bless you in ways you could have never imagined." Alicia decided to use the loss of Azilee's things to bless her with new ones.

Alicia decided she'd have a "Boutique Bargain Bash" for Azilee and her family. She'd get all of the girls at her school to donate their cute, but no longer worn outfits and shoes to Azilee and her family. Alicia wanted to have a party and the entrance fee would be the donation of cute attire, but the family could also benefit from any monetary donations that party goers offered. Alicia believed the superficial girls at the school would love her idea, and the party would be their reward for their good deed. She just had to see if her mom and dad would love it as much.

Surprisingly, Alicia's mom and dad gave the all clear to have the party. So, the next day at school, Alicia spread the word like crazy. She wanted everyone to come and she wanted them to bring clothes for everyone in Azilee's family, so they'd have to get clothes from their parents and siblings too.

As Alicia was party planning with some of her friends, Kevin Giddons walked up and put in his two cents. "So, you taking up clothes for country bumpkin Azilee, huh? 'Bout time somebody showed that girl how to dress."

He laughed at his own rude joke expecting everyone else to laugh, too. When no one laughed, Alicia took it upon herself to correct Kevin. "Kevin, do you remember when we were in the fifth grade?"

"Yeah, why?" he asked puzzled by Alicia's out of the blue question.

"Well, I remember it too, and I think a lot of the girls here remember it."

"And?"

"Well, as I remember it, you were about five inches shorter than most of the girls here, and you had to wear your older brother's hand-me-downs that were still too long for you. You looked like a sack of bones. And, with those glasses on, you looked like a skeleton with an eye problem." Alicia high-fived one of her friends and the group laughed hysterically.

"Well, I couldn't help that my eyes were jacked up back then."

"And they'd be jacked up now, too, if you didn't wear those contact lenses. Fake, phony-baloney!"

The group was in stiches at Alicia's jokes. Even Alicia had to chuckle, she didn't know she had it in her to be so funny, and to put someone in their place all at the same time, in defense of someone else. But, she was doing it quite well. In a huff, Kevin left, too embarrassed to say anything else.

"Well, I guess we won't have to worry about Kevin coming to the bash," Alicia laughed. All of the girls continued with the party planning, excited about the whole event. Later that evening, Alicia received a strange phone call. It was Kevin. He was trying to make small talk, but to Alicia, it was obvious that he wanted to apologize, but he couldn't come right out and say it, so Alicia helped him out.

"Kevin, you never call me. Let's be honest. Do you want to apologize for the rude things you said about Azilee?"
Sheepishly, Kevin replied, "Yes."

"Well, the best way to apologize is to come to the Bash and bring plenty of GOOD clothes for Azilee and her family." Alicia emphasized the word, good, to make sure Kevin was clear on what he was expected to do. Otherwise, he might bring old, ragged, and unusable clothes, thinking he was doing a good deed.

"Alright, I can do that." After a long pause, Kevin asked, "Hey, do you think Azilee will come to the party?"

"I don't know. I told her mom to tell her about it the other day, when they came by their old house, but I don't know."

"Well, if she does come, I want to apologize to her," Kevin admitted.

"I think she'd like that. She's still our neighbor, and she needs all the support and friends she can get right now. And, after all the mess you've put her through, you'd better be really nice to her."

"Alright. I get it. No one is perfect, even me." They both laughed, but Kevin was the one who found the right words. "I will make sure to think about people's feelings, from now on. It didn't feel good when you brought up my past, so I know it doesn't feel good to Azilee to hear the things I've said to her."

"Now, you get it. We've all been a little wrong when it comes to Azilee, but I think it took this tragedy to make us realize that we have to do as the Bible says, and love our neighbor, as we love ourselves."

"So basically, we have to treat people the way we want to be treated, and everything will be cool."

"Yeah, Kevin," Alicia giggled at nothing in particular, just the good feeling she felt because both she and Kevin were finally doing something good for Azilee instead of hurting her.

"Yep, everything will be cool." Kevin added, also pleased to be doing something good for their neighbor.

Discussion Questions

(Discuss your thoughts with an adult or peer mentor.)

1. Why do you think it was so easy for Alicia to act snobby towards Azilee about the fashion magazine?

2. What do you think made Alicia want to apologize to Azilee?

3. When Alicia mentioned the vain girls would need to receive something for their good deed, what does that say about some people?

4. Is it better to give something to someone be it a smile, hug, gifts, or charity, or is it better to receive? Why?

5. Why did Alicia choose to confront Kevin the way that she did by embarrassing him?

6. Why did Kevin want to help Azilee in the end? Why do you think it took this to make him want to help?

7. Have you ever been picked on or have you ever picked on someone else? Explain.

8. How did it make you feel to be picked on, or how did it make you feel to pick on someone else?

9. Why should we treat people the way we want to be treated?

10. Pretend to be Azilee. How would you feel if her situation happened to you? (i.e. being teased, being misunderstood, and losing your home)

Chapter Fourteen

Choosing Sides

After school, Raina, Gia, and April sat comfortably in their regular booth at Smokin' Burgers. Gia smacked her gum, as she maneuvered the salt and pepper shakers on the table, until they were extremely close together. She was trying to show Raina and April how close their friend Kaylen had been standing next to Shawn, the star of the basketball team, earlier that day.

"I told you she liked him. I could tell by the way she was passing notes to him in class," Gia informed her attentive audience. Or, at least she thought they were anxious to hear her story. Raina hadn't liked how Gia had been talking about their friend, Kaylen, for months now, and it seemed to just be getting worse. She knew she'd have to say something soon, or things would get really nasty.

"She's always trying to get a boyfriend," Gia huffed. She just needs to stop being so desperate."

Raina couldn't hold her tongue any longer. "Gia, Kaylen's our friend. If she wants to talk to Shawn, what's the problem?"

"What's the problem?" Gia snapped. "The problem is, she's going to make herself look like a loser, and I don't hang out with losers."

"Well, whatever she does, we're her friends," Raina shrugged, "and it feels funny talking about her behind her back."

April remained quiet. She didn't agree with Raina or Gia. She just kept dipping her fries into ketchup.

Gia rolled her eyes and smacked her gum again, thinking. "Well," she finally said, "I still say, she needs to watch it, or something bad might happen."

Raina and April both looked at Gia with surprise. That sounded like a threat.

"You mean she could end up getting her feelings hurt by Shawn, right? Raina asked for clarification.

"I mean ... Yeah, that's ... that's what I mean." Gia said without looking Raina in the eye.

Still quiet, April was satisfied with that answer, and went from dipping her fries to taking a bite out of her burger. Raina, on the other hand, was not at all satisfied with the tone of Gia's answer, but decided to just let it go.

****

The rain pounded Gia's mom's car, and the windshield wipers were working overtime, and so did the girls' voices. Raina and Gia had to talk loudly, to be heard over the rain. The girls had known that it would rain, when they planned to go to the movies, but they had been waiting for months for the movie's release, so rain or snow storm, they were determined to go.

It was going to be just the four of them, Raina, Gia, April, and Kaylen. April and Kaylen were coming from different parts of the city, so they were meeting Gia and Raina. When Gia's mom dropped them off in front of the theater, they quickly grabbed an umbrella from the backseat, and hurriedly took shelter in the theater's lobby.

After Raina and Gia bought their tickets, they turned to see April waving to them from the concession stand. Making their way over to April, they spoke to numerous girls and guys who attended their school. The girls made their purchases and started in the direction of their movie, until Raina reminded them that Kaylen hadn't shown up yet.

Rolling her eyes, Gia made a comment about Kaylen's tardiness, but agreed to wait for her to show up. Fifteen minutes later, the girls were about to give up and go into the movie when Kaylen showed up smiling as though nothing was wrong. The frown on all of the girls' faces told her otherwise.

"Hey, girls! What's wrong?" Kaylen asked, strolling closer.

Without skipping a beat, Gia snapped, "We've been waiting for you, and now we're going to miss the beginning of the movie. What a waste!"

"You told me the movie started at eight, Gia. Remember?"

"No, I didn't say that." Gia looked away.

Kaylen's eyes narrowed as she checked out the other girls and came to another conclusion. "And, Gia, you told me we were all going to wear white tonight. Nobody's wearing white, but me, and now I have mud and water spots on my new white jeans because of all of this rain."

"You must've gotten it wrong again. I never told you we were all wearing white. We all knew it was going to rain tonight. It would make no sense to say we're all wearing white."

"Well, whether or not it made sense, you said you had talked to the other girls, and that's what we were going to do."

Waiting for Gia to answer proved useless, when she shrugged and turned away. Raina and April had stood by, speechless, while their friends went back and forth, but now they agreed that it was time to enter the movie. Knowing that arguing wasn't going to make things any better, Kaylen decided to cut her losses and just head into the movie before they missed any more of it.

Although tensions were in the air, the girls managed to enjoy the movie, and at the end, said their goodbyes and promised to call each other the next day.

****

When Kaylen unexpectedly showed up on Raina's doorstep on Saturday morning, a sleepy-eyed Raina was in disbelief of the information Kaylen brought with her. Coming through the door, Raina swore that she hadn't logged on to her social media accounts yet that morning, but according to Kaylen, Gia had posted a picture of Kaylen online. The ugly timeline picture came complete with derogatory names and other unflattering pictures. When Kaylen had confronted Gia about it earlier that morning, she had said her account had been hacked, but Kaylen wasn't buying it.

"So, if you don't think her account was hacked, why do you think she posted that stuff about you online?" Raina shook her head in disbelief.

"Because, I found out from Shawn last night, after the movies, that Gia tried to talk to him, but he turned her down. She's been acting strangely towards him ever since. And, now that he likes me, she just can't take it."

"Did you ask her about all of that?"

"I tried, but after I confronted her about the stuff she said last night, she just hung up." Kaylen was in tears now. "I don't understand, Raina, why did she have to do that to me? I thought we were friends. I didn't even know she liked Shawn. Why didn't she just talk to me about it?"

"I don't know," Raina told her, truthfully. "I don't know," she repeated, "but, I'm going to find out right now." Kaylen followed her upstairs to her room.

Once the door was closed, Raina logged on to her Face Place account. Sure enough, there was a horrible picture of Kaylen, with those horrible words, and the pictures she had described. It was sickening. Especially, coming from someone that they both had considered a friend.

Gia hadn't posted from her regular account. Instead, she'd posted from an anonymous account – one that she'd believed would be untraceable. Over the last few months, Gia had used the account to post mean things about other girls, and now she was posting about Kaylen. Raina had disagreed with Gia's choice to post those things, and Gia promised she'd stop. Apparently, she hadn't.

This time, Raina wasn't going to let it slide.

She picked up her phone and speed dialed Gia. It was early in the morning, but with something like this, there was no time to waste. Gia answered the phone in her sleepiest voice ever, but Raina was determined to get some answers. She knew she was awake because Kaylen had confronted her earlier that morning.

"Stop playing, Gia! This is no game. Why did you post those lies about Kaylen online?"

"What are you talking about? I already told her my account was hacked. I don't know who posted that stuff about her. Anyway, from what I heard, it's true. But, you shouldn't even worry about all that. You should be worried about how this is making you look ... being her friend and all."

Angry, Raina was starting to feel like steam was coming from the top of her head. "You know, just like I know, the things you posted online about Kaylen are not true." The other end of the phone line grew quiet, but Raina continued, "Gia, I didn't realize that you liked Shawn; none of us did. Is that what this is all about?"

"What? If I wanted Shawn, he'd be mine," Gia laughed.

"Well, why'd you do it?"

"Look, the stuff that's online about Kaylen is the truth, and she knows it. And Raina, I did put it online, but she deserves it."

"How did she deserve it?" Raina asked.

"She just does. I gotta go; I'll call you later." Gia hung up the phone.

"Well, at least she confessed." Still holding the phone, Raina looked at Kaylen and said, "I still can't believe it, but she did it."

Both girls plopped down on the bed. Kaylen, with a puzzled look on her face, questioned, "So what do we do now?"

"I don't know yet, but I do know, that right now, I can't call her my friend. Friends don't do this to friends."

Both girls looked at each other in silence and then at the computer in an attempt to figure out how to clean up the colossal mess that Gia had made. Raina finally realized that she could no longer play the Girl in the Middle between her friends. She had to finally choose sides.

Discussion and Questions

According to dosomething.com, approximately forty-three percent of kids have been bullied online. Seventy percent of students say that they frequently see bullying online. Girls are about twice as likely as boys to be victims and perpetrators of cyber bullying.

Cyberbullying can have deadly consequences with many victims committing suicide to escape the constant harassment. To combat this tragedy, there are various laws that outline the specific consequences for cyberbullying in each state of the U.S. Keeping these facts in mind, please discuss your thoughts about the following questions with an adult or peer mentor.

1. What do you think Raina and Kaylen should do?

2. Instead of posting bad things online about Kaylen, how could Gia have handled her feelings toward Kaylen?

3. Have you ever experienced cyber bullying?

4. How do you think this situation will end?

5. Why is it important not to participate in cyber bullying either as the bully or an encouraging bystander?

6. Why is important to choose sides when a friend gets out of control?

7. What does the "Girl Code or Guy Code" mean to you?

8. When is it worth keeping the "Girl Code or Guy Code?" Why?

Chapter Fifteen

Coded 2!

Use the characters below to decode the sayings.

A=☺☺ B=≠ C=⟁ D=π E=ə F=≥ G=± H=£ I=¥ J=⚡ K=◊ L=ꙍ M=Λ
N=⅋ O=□ P=ẑ Q=● R=⊢ S=◯ T=ʒ U=ᵥ V=∫ W=↓ X=↕ Y=∏ Z=₪

≠ ᵥ ꙍ ꙍ∏¥⅋±   ¥◯   ≥□ᵥꙍ

B U L L Y I N G   I S   F O U L

☺☺ꙍ↓☺☺∏□   £ə ꙍ◯ẑ   □ʒ£ə⊢◯

A L W A Y S   H E L P   O T H E R S

☺☺ꙍ↓☺☺∏□   ʒ£¥⅋◊   ẑ□◯¥ʒ¥∫ə

A L W A Y S   T H I N K   P O S I T I V E

☺☺ꙍ↓☺☺∏□   ◯ʒ⊢¥∫ə   ≥□⊢   ±⊢ə☺☺ʒ⅋ə◯◯

A L W A Y S   S T R I V E   F O R   G R E A T N E S S

☺☺ꙍ↓☺☺∏□   ꙍ□∫ə   □ʒ£ə⊢◯

A L W A Y S   L O V E   O T H E R S

79

Chapter Sixteen

Who have I become?

Choosing sides is not always easy. Sometimes a football team that seems to be winning at first, ends up losing the game because of one very bad mistake. Some mistakes can be erased, but others have consequences that can change the course of your entire life in an unfavorable way. Whenever you make a decision, choose the side that will help you to become the best person you can be. After all, who wants to be on a losing team?
Since you have read the stories and completed the activities in this book, evaluate what you have learned about yourself. With an adult or peer mentor, honestly answer the questions that follow.

1.   What will I change about my outlook on life?

2.   If I need to control my temper, what are some ways I can control it?

3.   What is the best thing to do when someone angers me?

4.   How can I help others?

5.   What should I do if I see someone else doing wrong?

6.   Am I a good friend? Why or why not?

7.   Do I care if I make enemies? Why or why not?

8.   Do I treat others the way I want to be treated? Why or why not?

9. Can I find positive role models to be examples of positive behavior? If so, who are they and why are they positive?

10. Is it cool to be disrespectful? Please explain why or why not?

11. What do I plan to do with my life?

12. What values do I share with my friends?

13. What am I willing to sacrifice or nurture for friendship? Is this good for me? For my friends?

14. What traits make up a man or woman of quality?

15. Do I have those traits? If not, what do I need to do to develop them?

16. Have I learned anything in this workbook that will change the way I speak or act?

17. Everyone learns from watching someone. Who am I watching and who is watching me?

18. Which side do I choose: to be a great person or a person who lives on the opposite side of greatness?

Reference

"11 Facts About Cyber Bullying." DoSomething.org. N.p., n.d. Web. 05 Oct 2016.

Special thanks to:
Gail McFarland, Editor
Osmond Curtis, Book Interior Designer
Desmaine Cousin, Cover Designer

Made in the USA
Columbia, SC
10 November 2018